THE EPISTLES OF JOHN

Walking in Truth · Love · Light

A Pastoral Commentary on 1-3 John

by Joseph Edwards-Hoff

Copyright

ISBN 978-1-971665-01-6

Published by

Joseph Edwards-Hoff

Grandview, Washington

Printed in the United States of America

Dedication

To the saints of Revival Church,

"I have no greater joy than to hear that my children walk in truth."

This commentary is dedicated to you—not merely because it is written for you, but because it has been formed among you. You have walked with me verse by verse through the Word of God, listening, asking, and laboring together to apply His truth to our lives.

Your steadfastness, hunger for the Word, and love for Christ have been an encouragement not only to me, but to many. It is my prayer that God will continue to use our church body to stir others likewise to seek Christ and to walk faithfully before Him.

I pray that you will continue to walk in the truth, and if you wander, that Christ will quickly bring you home. I pray that He will be magnified in us in all that we do. And I pray that you will finish your race well, hearing those blessed words, "Well done, good and faithful servant," and that the Word of God will continue to dwell richly among us.

About the Author

Joseph Edwards-Hoff is the pastor of Revival Church in Grandview, Washington, where he serves with a deep commitment to the local church, expository preaching, and the authority of God's Word. His ministry has been shaped not only by years of teaching and shepherding, but by the daily realities of leading a church, raising a family, and laboring to finish well.

Joseph's teaching emphasizes careful attention to the biblical text, historical context, and theological clarity, with a consistent focus on faithful application. He believes the truths of Scripture are meant to shape real lives in real churches, and that doctrine divorced from obedience ultimately fails the Church it claims to serve.

He is married to his wife, Nicole, and together they are raising their seven children. Much of Joseph's pastoral theology has been formed in the ordinary, often unseen work of family life and local church ministry, where faithfulness is tested not in theory, but in practice.

How to Use This Commentary

This commentary is written for anyone who loves the Word of God and wants to understand it more clearly and live it more faithfully—it is not written only for those in ministry, nor does it assume formal theological training.

The New King James Version (NKJV) is used by default unless otherwise noted. Greek words are included at times where they help clarify meaning, though no prior knowledge of Greek is needed. These word studies are meant to serve the reader and deepen understanding.

Historical background, grammar, and theology are addressed to help the reader better understand what the text is actually saying and how that truth is meant to be lived out. Illustrations and pastoral observations are included to show how sound doctrine is meant to shape real obedience.

The material in this commentary was first taught in my church and then adapted from sermons there. Because of that, the chapters follow the flow of those teachings rather than strict chapter divisions. Some sections receive more extended attention while others are treated more briefly, allowing certain themes to be developed carefully and, at times, revisited.

The historical and theological context is presented as it arose in those sermons, and so introductory material is found both at the beginning of 1 John and again in the opening of 3 John.

In the end, the aim of this commentary is not information, but transformation—so that Christ would be more clearly seen, loved, and followed.

Table of Contents

Fellowship, Light, & Confession
1 John 1:1-10

This epistle was written near AD 100, in the late 90s. One commentator made an insightful observation about John 1:1 in the Gospel—'In the beginning was the word and the word was with God and the word was God'—and compared it with 1 John 1:1, 'that which was from the beginning.' He noted how John had a remarkable grasp of the eternal nature of God, surpassing even the other gospel writers and much of Paul's writings. John seemed to truly comprehend this eternal perspective.

This observation provides one more reason to hold the minority position that John composed the book of Revelation first, followed by his Gospel and then the epistles. Most scholars propose an earlier date for the Gospel of John, possibly in the AD 70s or 80s, with Revelation dated to AD 95. However, the early church did not extensively discuss the dating of John's Gospel or epistles. The earliest mention by any early church father—not appearing until the fifth century—indicates that Revelation came first, then the Gospel, and finally the epistles.

This sequence makes theological sense. If Jesus appeared to John on Patmos and revealed all the visions of Revelation, those experiences would naturally inform his subsequent writings—both the Gospel and the epistles. The emphasis on 'that which was from the beginning' reflects a view of God that would be uniquely shaped by the Revelation experience. John would have undergone a transformation that fundamentally changed his understanding, giving him insights the other gospel writers did not possess.

Lastly, it can be clearly seen that a major theme found in John's gospel, as well as in this epistle, is that of love. In the Book of Revelation Jesus tells John to write seven letters to seven churches. The first church addressed is the Church of Ephesus, which happens to be the church which John was the pastor of. The one complaint that Jesus had about that church was their lack of love, and so it seems fitting that after hearing this John would emphasize love in all of his writings.

Addressing Early Church Heresy

John wrote this epistle to address the false teachings that began circulating in the early church. Many of these heresies are the very issues that the Council of Nicaea in AD 325 sought to address, and they appear as concerns throughout various New Testament epistles.

Judaizers appear throughout the New Testament—in Acts, in Galatians, and in nearly every one of Paul's epistles. These were Jews or their followers who insisted that Gentiles must essentially become Jewish and keep the law. They were the lawkeepers.

Antinomians represented the opposite extreme. The Greek word for law is *nomos*, so "anti-*nomos*" means "against the law." These were the lawbreakers who taught that since believers are no longer under the law, they can do whatever they want. Grace, in their view, meant complete freedom from any moral constraint. This was an early church issue, and it remains one today. Interestingly, both the Judaizers and Antinomians persist in various forms, with flavors of Judaizing appearing in movements like Seventh-day Adventism and the Hebrew Roots movement, depending on how deeply adherents embrace law-keeping and Sabbath observance.

Gnosticism taught that a divine spark created all things. Gnostics developed their own creation account, claiming that this divine spark is purely spiritual. Therefore, they reasoned, all things spiritual are good, all good things are spiritual, and all matter is evil. This is why they denied that Jesus had a physical body—since Jesus was obviously spiritual, He could not have been material. The classic illustration often used is that if Jesus walked on the beach, He would not leave footprints. That is what they taught.

Gnosticism had subgroups. Because matter is evil, two opposing movements emerged. Asceticism taught believers to deny the flesh. Paul addresses this extensively in Colossians and elsewhere. Since the flesh is evil, ascetics believed you should fast, live in rags, and torture your body to kill the flesh. Some Gnostics promoted this extreme self-denial.

Other sects embraced **Hedonism**—the idea that you can do whatever your flesh wants because the flesh is evil and therefore not the real you. The real you is the spiritual part, so whatever you do in your flesh does not really matter. These competing philosophies circulated throughout the early church.

More specific heresies emerged from these broader movements. **Docetism** taught that Jesus was purely spirit with no human body. The Docetists were the specific group denying Christ's physical incarnation.

Cerinthianism, named after a man named Cerinthus, was part of the Gnostic movement. This heresy taught that Jesus was sometimes divine. According to this view, He was born as just a man, but upon His baptism, He was endued with the power and spirit of God and essentially took on deity. At the crucifixion, He lost His deity and became merely a man again. We will be referring back to him repeatedly throughout this commentary due to his relevance to this epistle.

Marcionism taught that the Old Testament God was different from the New Testament God. This idea still surfaces today in various forms, but it was a real teaching that people actively promoted in the early centuries.

Arianism was the main point of debate at the Council of Nicaea. This heresy taught that Jesus was a created being— not the immortal, eternal God. This is one of the biggest heresies that truly separates Christians from the cults. When Jesus is merely a created being with a beginning, we are talking about a different Jesus entirely. That is a serious matter.

Sabellianism, more commonly called **Modalism**, denies the Trinity. This heresy teaches that God the Father, when He became Jesus, put a 'do not disturb' sign on heaven's gate and came down as Jesus. When Jesus prayed to the Father, there was no one up there—He was just praying to Himself. Nobody was home; it was the answering machine. Then when Jesus ascended into heaven, He came back as the Holy Spirit. This is the idea of not three persons but one God in three forms or modes.

We speak of the three persons of the Trinity because we see interaction within the Godhead. Scripture reveals distinct personalities who interact with each other and with us. This is why we say 'God in three persons, blessed Trinity'— because it does not make biblical sense that God left heaven and became Jesus, then turned from Jesus into the Holy Spirit. Yet this heresy persists even in some churches today.

These are the heresies that were circulating in John's day. When you understand these false teachings, John's writings become clearer. You begin to recognize why he is so specific about certain things—he is addressing teachings his readers were familiar with and needed to combat.

That Which Was from the Beginning

> *"That which was from the beginning, which we have heard, which we have seen with our eyes, which we have looked upon, and our hands have handled, concerning the Word of life" (1 John 1:1)*

John begins with 'that which was from the beginning,' echoing the opening of his Gospel. In John 1:1, he wrote, 'In the beginning was the Word.' That means when time started, the Word was already there. We need to remember that God exists outside of time. Consider what it takes to have a universe: you need three things. You need time, space, and matter. You need something—that is the matter. You need a place to put the matter—that is space. And you need a time to put it there—that is time. These three things must all exist simultaneously.

Genesis captures this beautifully: 'In the beginning'— time—'God created the heavens'—space—'and the earth'— matter. But John 1:1 tells us that in the beginning, when this happened, the Word *was*. Jesus was already there. Colossians makes it clear that all things were made through Him. So when John writes 'that which was from the beginning,' he is emphasizing Christ's eternal preexistence.

John continues: 'which we have heard, which we have seen with our eyes.' These verbs are in ongoing tenses. One translator put it this way: it is almost like John is saying, 'We heard and it is still ringing in our ears. We saw it with

5

our eyes, but those images are still there.' He is emphasizing the lasting impact that Jesus had on him.

'Which we have looked upon'—this phrase uses a unique Greek word, *theaomai* (θεάομαι), which means to look attentively, to contemplate, or to inspect. It means to look at something and really take it in. John must have stared at Jesus sometimes. Imagine what happens when Jesus looks over and catches you staring at Him—you probably look the other direction! But John is saying, 'I used to just stare at the guy. I used to just stare at Him and take Jesus in. This is the Word made flesh. This is God in human form.' And John just looked and contemplated.

He emphasizes further: 'Our hands have handled Him.' This directly counters the Gnostic heresy that Jesus was just spirit. John is saying, 'No, I have held Him. He has held me. When He said that one of us would betray Him, I laid my head back against His breast and asked, 'Is it me, Lord?' He told me, 'It is not you, John. You do not need to worry.' I have touched Him.'

All of this concerns 'the Word of life.' Life itself was embodied in Jesus Christ.

> *"The life was manifested, and we have seen,*
> *and bear witness, and declare to you that*
> *eternal life which was with the Father and*
> *was manifested to us" (1 John 1:2)*

The life—really life itself, the concept of life—was manifested for us. It was made visible for us. 'We have seen and bear witness and declare to you that eternal life which was with the Father.' This eternal life, this concept, this person, was with the Father, but then He was manifested to us.

6

The idea of being manifested is taking something that was not previously seen or known and making it seeable and knowable. In John 1:18, John wrote, 'No one has seen God at any time. The only begotten Son, who is in the bosom of the Father, He has declared Him.' He is saying the same thing here.

The word 'declared' is *exēgeomai* (ἐξηγέομαι). This is where we get our words 'exegesis' or 'exegete' from. In short, exegesis is what pastors ought to be doing—taking the Bible and exegeting it, going in and discovering what is there and digging it up and out so we can better understand it. What pastors sadly do too much of in the church these days is eisegesis, where they have an idea and try to find it in the Bible and put it in there. We are supposed to be digging truth out of the Bible. That is exegesis.

Jesus took God and made Him understandable. He brought out all the details so that we could see God. Colossians 1:15 says that Jesus 'is the image of the invisible God, the firstborn over all creation.' The word 'image' is the Greek word *eikon*. This is where we get 'icon' or 'idol' from. This might seem strange—calling Jesus an idol—but the idea was that the pagans could not see their gods, so what did they do? They built little statues so they could see their god.

Remember when Aaron made the golden calf? He did not say this calf's name is Bob or Molech or Ra. He said this calf is Yahweh. 'This is the Lord who brought you out of Egypt.' The people wanted to see God, so they made an icon, a molded image. But Jesus is a physical, tangible being that John and the disciples could see and behold, and now they could see God. No one had seen God at any time, but now they see God and are able to understand Him.

7

If you want to know anything about God, look to Jesus. It is a very simple test. As we study the Bible and get to know Jesus better and better, sometimes people have biblical questions, and the simple answer is: Could you see Jesus doing that? 'Well, no.' Well, there you go then. Is it okay for us to do this in church? Could you imagine Jesus doing that in church? No. Well, there you go then. What do you think God says? Look to Jesus, and you will have God's perfect reflection so that we can see it.

Another description of Jesus talks about Him being like the molding from a cast, like a die. You press it in—like those wax seals—and you have the seal, but the image left behind is Jesus. If you took God and made a mold, there is Jesus. He was manifested for us.

All of this said, John was probably upset because he knew Jesus. He might have been one of the last people alive at this time who had met Jesus. And when people start saying that Jesus is something that He is not, the old son of thunder probably got stirred up again. The more real Jesus is to us, the more we will be upset when people misrepresent Him, and it will have an impact on our lives. Jesus should be manifested to us—a real, tangible experience in our lives. We might not see Him in the flesh like John did, but we have seen the definite changes in our lives because of Him. He has made Himself very known.

> *"That which we have seen and heard we declare to you, that you also may have fellowship with us; and truly our fellowship is with the Father and with His Son Jesus Christ" (1 John 1:3)*

John shifts focus: 'That which we have seen and heard'—and again, those things are still ringing in our ears—'we now declare to you.' This is the idea of making disciples and evangelism at its core. It is not only about going out and preaching on the street corner or knocking door to door, but it is what you have experienced that you then declare to others. They see what is in you, and they desire that, and you just declare to them what you have seen and what you have heard.

John says, 'That you also may have fellowship with us. And truly our fellowship is with the Father and with His Son Jesus Christ.' That is what we want. We want people to see in us our fellowship with God. And then we tell them, 'You can have fellowship with us, but our fellowship is with God.' We are drawing people in.

This word 'fellowship' is *koinōnia* (κοινωνία). Perhaps you have heard this word before. Chuck Missler's ministry was called Koinonia House. *Koinōnia* is also translated as association, community, communion, joint participation, intimacy, and intercourse. The whole concept speaks of a very unified, brought-together connection—*koinōnia*. It is the word used for communion.

> *"The cup of blessing which we bless, is it*
> *not the communion of the blood of Christ?*
> *The bread which we break, is it not the*
> *communion of the body of Christ?" (1 Cor.*
> *10:16)*

In John 6, Jesus was talking about how His flesh is food indeed and His blood is drink indeed: 'You need to eat My flesh; you need to drink My blood.' Part of this, in their culture, was understanding that they were assimilating this into their body. If I ate something, it is becoming a part of me. This is why dietary and food laws were so important to the Jews—there was a lot built into their understanding of eating food and what that means.

9

When you eat with other people, you are both sharing in that meal. It was an intimate thing. You did not eat with tax collectors and sinners. When we hear about Jesus eating with tax collectors and sinners, it might seem casual to us, but to a Jew, that had specific connotations. That means you are joining in an intimate act with these people— something you would not normally do. Jews would only ever eat with Jews.

We see Peter getting called out by Paul at Antioch because when the Jews from Jerusalem showed up, Peter pulled away from eating with the Gentiles and went back to eating just with Jews. Paul calls him out: 'We do not do that anymore. That is not our deal.' But this *koinōnia*, this fellowship, as we take communion, is something reminding us that we are becoming one with Christ. And therefore, if I am one with Christ and you are one with Christ, then we are one with one another. And every believer across the globe is part of that.

> *"There is one body and one Spirit, just as*
> *you were called in one hope of your calling;*
> *one Lord, one faith, one baptism; one God*
> *and Father of all, who is above all, and*
> *through all, and in you all" (Eph. 4:4-6)*

John is emphasizing this communion that we have with each other because of our communion with Christ.

> *"And these things we write to you that your*
> *joy may be full" (1 John 1:4)*

The transition from verse 4 into verse 5 and beyond is crucial. These things we have been talking about—the real manifestation of Jesus in our lives, that feeling of His presence, that feeling of His nearness—lead to fullness of joy. During those times when it feels like He is there with us, when there is this fellowship and this communion with Him and He is being manifested in our lives, our joy is full.

John moves from verse 5 all the way through the end of chapter 2 talking about the things that will steal that joy from us. Sin will break that fellowship. The penalty for sin has been paid. As a Christian, we do not need to worry about being kicked out of heaven, but we do need to worry about sin affecting our relationship with God. And when our relationship with God is not going well, things are not great.

Two things are true. First, my wife Nicole will never divorce me. I am not putting her to the test, but I do not think she will leave me because I think she is committed just like I am committed to our relationship and our marriage. I have full assurance that I am going to die a married man. On the flip side, there is a whole lot of stuff I can do that messes up our relationship. And sometimes it is not very fun. I can mess up our relationship. I can make her angry. I can disappoint her. I can break her heart. I have no fear that she is divorcing me over these things, but the joy of our marriage goes away when I am living in such a way that grieves my wife.

This is what John is talking about as he gets into confession and walking in the light. He is trying to bring that point home. He did not write this to unbelievers to win them to the faith. He wrote this to believers so that they would not break that fellowship with God, so that they would not lose that *koinōnia*, so that the manifestation of God in their life would always be there and their joy would be full.

It is recognizing that as we confess our sins and get real with God, we can start working on our relationship again. It is the same with your spouse. If you do not admit that you are wrong, usually that argument lasts a lot longer than

11

when you just fess up, say you are sorry, and work through it and move on. It is the same with God. He wants our joy to be full, and so He is tying together obedience and joy.

'That your joy may be full' is a phrase Jesus used more than once on the night of the Last Supper.

> *"As the Father loved Me, I also have loved you; abide in My love. If you keep My commandments, you will abide in My love, just as I have kept My Father's commandments and abide in His love. These things I have spoken to you, that My joy may remain in you, and that your joy may be full" (John 15:9-11)*

Jesus is giving us context here. As He has been doing, abide in His love. Walk like Jesus walked, as 1 John 2:6 says. It is very simple. We are in a relationship. We know that there are things that will grieve your spouse, your parents, your friends. And if you do those things, it hinders your relationship. But if you avoid those bad things and even proactively do the good things, then your relationship thrives.

This is not about obedience in some weird, heavy, legalistic way. This is Jesus talking. This is the apostle whom Jesus loved talking. And they are talking about working out your relationship with the Lord. He wants your joy to be full. All these things He is telling us to do—when we do not do them, they hurt God. They hurt us. They hurt other people. This is why God calls them sin and tells us not to do them.

> *"Therefore you now have sorrow; but I will see you again and your heart will rejoice, and your joy no one will take from you. And in that day you will ask Me nothing. Most assuredly, I say to you, whatever you ask the*

Father in My name He will give you. Until
now you have asked nothing in My name.
Ask, and you will receive, that your joy may
be full" (John 16:22-24)

Jesus is looking ahead to the crucifixion. He is going to be arrested that night and crucified the next day, and He is saying there is going to be sorrow. Already He has said one of them will betray Him, and they are going to take Him. The disciples are having a shockful night of all the things Jesus is saying, so they are sorrowful. But Jesus says, 'I am going to see you again at the resurrection, and then you are going to rejoice to see the risen Lord. And in that day you will ask Me nothing'—because you will just be there with Jesus, and everything is going to be great.

'But there is going to come a time where you are going to have fellowship with the Father and you can ask Him things and talk to God. And if you ask it in God's will, you are going to have it. If it is going to be in My name and according to My heart and My desire, you are going to have those things. There is going to be a relationship going in that day, and your joy will be filled.' Again, this is looking toward that relationship, having that relationship with God. 'You will have communion with the Father. I might be gone, but you are still going to have communion with Me. And there is going to be this back-and-forth and conversation and talking.'

He emphasizes these things so that our joy may be full.

Walking in the Light

"This is the message which we have heard
from Him and declare to you, that God is
light and in Him is no darkness at all. If we
say that we have fellowship with Him, and

13

> *walk in darkness, we lie and do not practice*
> *the truth. But if we walk in the light as He is*
> *in the light, we have fellowship with one*
> *another, and the blood of Jesus Christ His*
> *Son cleanses us from all sin" (1 John 1:5-7)*

The reality is that we know there is something wrong if we are walking in darkness. Sadly, there are a lot of people in this world who might say they believe in God or that they are a Christian, but if you look at their walk, it does not reflect it. John is being real with his readers, and it is important for us to be real with them. First John is a good place to take people and just see what the Word of God does.

We can say to someone, 'I know you say you believe in God, but even the demons believe and tremble, as James said. And you are walking in darkness. You are not really walking in the light. You are not really obeying what God says. And if that is the truth, then we lie and we do not practice the truth.'

But then there is that promise: 'If we walk in the light as He is in the light, we have fellowship with one another, and the blood of Jesus Christ His Son cleanses us from all sin.' This is a great verse to explain to your friends and family and whoever else. Walk in the light. Be like Jesus. Do these things. This is good stuff. Quit walking that way and start walking for Him. And the blood of Jesus Christ His Son will cleanse us of all sin.

This is a good reminder that it is all sin—past, present, and future. When you get saved, He says, 'I am giving you eternal life. It is life everlasting.' Once we enter into that eternal life, we have eternal life. He has forgiven us of everything. What we cannot do is mess that up. If we have really received eternal life, then that eternal life is eternal.

There are verses telling us that God gives us eternal life. There is never a verse that talks about God taking eternal life away. There are all these verses promising what He is going to give us, and we never see the opposite. We read about being born again. The Bible is silent on becoming dead again. It just is not there. It is a good theological conversation to have, and we can divide things and go through it. But the idea is that we do see 'born again' as a concept again and again. We never see 'dead again.' You were brought from death to life. You were spiritually dead; now you are made spiritually alive.

Now what? Well, you have been given eternal life. The emphasis for us is that even if we cannot lose our salvation, we can really mess up our relationship with God. We can mess up our eternal reward. We can mess up a whole lot of things. And we can get to a deep, dark place. But if we have received the grace of God, it will be with us.

One of the greatest examples is in 1 Corinthians 3, where it talks about Jesus Christ being the foundation. There is no other foundation which any man may lay. If you build upon it with wood, hay, and stubble or metal and precious stones, when it is tested by fire, if everything lasts, you are getting rewarded. But if all burns up, it says that person will still enter—smelling like smoke, by the hair of their chinny-chin-chin. They are going to get in there, but they still enter because that foundation was laid, which is Christ.

We can lose a lot by living foolishly. So what is the best thing to do? It is to seek the Lord. It is to seek the Lord and confess our sins. So many believers—this is a plague in the church—have their growth stunted because of pride and their unwillingness to just call sin sin in their life. They want to call it 'the way I am.' They want to call it a bad habit. They want to call it anything else rather than just saying, 'God, this is sin, and I just need to call it sin, and I

15

need to repent of it. And when I do it again tomorrow, I need to call it sin again tomorrow, and I just need to keep coming before God calling sin sin and confessing these things.'

People give up on confession. They give up on taking these things before the Lord. And what it does is it hinders our relationship. It stunts our growth. It steals our joy. If you have a continual sin problem—maybe it is rudeness, maybe it is laziness and unfaithfulness, maybe it is something else that is not one of the 'big things'—God is trying to work out perfection in you. He is going to get the little things. You get past the big things, and He is going to start working out the little things. But whatever those things are, they will affect our relationship. And honestly, we usually feel guilty. It makes us feel guilty. It makes us feel ashamed when we realize that we really should not be doing this, but we keep on doing this.

> *"If we say that we have no sin, we deceive ourselves, and the truth is not in us. If we confess our sins, He is faithful and just to forgive us our sins and to cleanse us from all unrighteousness. If we say that we have not sinned, we make Him a liar, and His word is not in us" (1 John 1:8-10)*

If we confess our sins, He is faithful and just. That is a beautiful thing. He is the faithful one to cleanse us from those sins and to forgive us. We get it all. We get forgiveness—we do not need to feel guilty. And we get that cleansing work in our lives as we keep taking things before the Lord and allowing Him to continue to refine us and refine us and refine us.

You are never going to find someone who is sinless. Even people who from the outside do not seem like they have weaknesses—trust me, they do. God is going to do a refining process in these people. If we are seeking God as the Bible tells us to, if we are really living the life the Bible tells Christians we ought to live, if we start living as revived Christians, living out biblical Christianity—not the average everyday Christianity we see so much of today, but we are on fire for Jesus—you are going to find that yes, many of the sins of commission will fade far into the distance. Those are the things we do but should not do, like saying bad words or thinking bad thoughts or doing bad things.

But you are going to find that God is still going to be spending a long time refining those sins of omission—the things we know we should be doing and we really just do not do enough of. That is sin also. God says, 'Do not steal.' Therefore, if you steal, it is sin. But God also says, 'Pray without ceasing.' God also says to love one another. He says to give. He says to care. These are all things that when we are not doing those things, we are in sin.

It is not hard any day just to stop and look back over the past few hours and just pray, 'Lord, search me and know me, because I do not know me, but You do. Try my heart. See if there are any anxieties, any wicked way within me, and tell me about it so that I can confess it.' And He will start talking to you. You just give Him the opportunity, and you start realizing, 'That was kind of rude what I said there, was not it? Okay, that joke was funny, but it was probably hurtful. All right, Lord, I could have responded better in that situation. I am being lazy right now, and I am supposed to step up and be a man and lead my home and lead my family and love my wife.' And we can start confessing, 'All right, Lord, I confess those things to You. Those are sins. I need to change.'

17

And then you get back out there, and three hours later you have got more things to confess. But if we are living in such a way like that, just doing that promotes communion with God, fellowship with God, just talking to God more and more about things and just having an ongoing conversation. In the richest, most fulfilling, and joyful seasons—keyword: seasons—of my Christian life, I feel like I am talking to God all the time. It is just an ongoing conversation all the time. There is just continual redirecting and guiding my steps. My focus is on Him, and He is always keeping me where I need to be.

Verses 8 and 10 present the opposite perspective, and this is where many people are stuck. If we say we have no sin or that we have not sinned, God has an answer for that: we deceive ourselves, and the truth is not in us. We make Him a liar, and His word is not in us. It is a great reminder that anytime we feel like we do not have anything to repent of, we should take it before the Lord because there is a heart issue there.

Jesus Christ, Our Advocate
1 John 2:1-2

Our Advocate with the Father

> *"My little children, these things I write to*
> *you, so that you may not sin. And if anyone*
> *sins, we have an Advocate with the Father,*
> *Jesus Christ the righteous" (1 John 2:1)*

When you are in your late 90s, you can call everyone 'my little children' at that point. 'These things I write to you so that you may not sin. And if anyone sins, we have an Advocate with the Father, Jesus Christ the righteous.' This verse contains two great promises in one: the promise that you may not sin and the promise of forgiveness if we do sin.

We need to recognize that this is not a promise for sinless perfectionism—that you will never have any sin in your life that you need to repent of. If that were true, then verses 8 and 10 of the previous chapter would make no sense. Nor would the second half of this verse, where he says what to do when you sin. But there is a very practical promise here that God can help you with sin, and He can help you to stop sinning. He can help you be freed from the power of sin in your life.

What percentage of Christians today—actual born-again Christians, not just people who call themselves Christians—are actually experiencing the deliverance from sin that the Bible offers? The reality is it is probably not nearly as many as it should be.

Here in this verse, we have the word 'sin'—*hamartanō* (ἁμαρτάνω). This is the verb, the action to sin, to err, to miss the mark. Very literally, the bullseye is God—perfect light in which no darkness dwells. Anything even a smidgen off of that is sin. The bullseye is great. Even if you hit the green ring around the red circle, you are doing pretty good still, but that is still missing the bullseye. And that is the point. Sin is anything missing the mark.

This is getting into the Greek, but this is helpful for us. What John is saying here is in the aorist tense. This speaks of an action being done. So this is talking about acts of sin—that you may not commit acts of sin. This is in contrast to 1 John 3:6, which is in a present tense, meaning ongoing, habitual. We will look at that verse in just a second so we can contrast.

The voice is active. Greek has a way of having active, passive, and middle voices. Active means you are the one doing this. No one is making you do it—that would be passive. This is you. You are the one sinning. There is no one else to blame for this. And the mood is what is called subjunctive, which is the mood of possibility. And that is fitting because in this verse, 'that you may not sin'—well, it is a very sure possibility you will sin. It is going to be you actively the one sinning. And because it is an aorist, it is the idea that it is an act of sin.

> *"Whoever abides in Him does not sin.*
> *Whoever sins has neither seen Him nor*
> *known Him" (1 John 3:6)*

This verse sometimes confuses people. Again, this is where getting to the Greek is helpful. Both places here it is the same verb as we just looked at, but these are present tenses. A good translation would be: 'Whoever abides in Him does not continue in sin, and whoever is continuing in sin neither has seen Him nor known Him.' Walking speaks of an ongoing, continued action and direction. First John 3:6 is speaking of an ongoing, continued action and direction.

This is a good, fair warning for people. 'I am a Christian, but I am living with my boyfriend and we are not married.' 'I am a Christian, but I just get drunk three times a week.' 'I am a Christian, but I just swear like a sailor.' We are all works in progress, and Christians have been known to fornicate. Christians get drunk sometimes. Born-again people swear. The idea is that He will work these sins out of us. But when you see that in someone else, it is hard to say where their heart really is. What I am seeing is you walking in darkness. And the Bible warns that when we walk in darkness, the truth is not in us. Maybe you are deceiving yourself.

That is the sobering warning John is trying to give. But back to chapter 2, verse 1: 'I am writing these things to you so that you may not sin.' The Bible gives lots of instruction. Psalm 119 tells us, 'How can a young man cleanse his way? By taking heed according to Your word.' The Bible promises that if we get in the Word, the Word can help get us out of sin.

It was John Bunyan, the author of *The Pilgrim's Progress*, who said, 'This book will keep me from sin, or sin will keep me from this book.' And it is very true. Getting in the Word, getting in prayer, staying in fellowship with other believers—these things do help keep me from sin.

Another thing that helps keep me from sin is confessing my sin. You fall into a sin; you stumble. But if you stumble and you keep it to yourself, there is always this temptation to stumble again. Why? Well, because no one knows. And what is one hidden sin versus two hidden sins? Or what is

21

five hidden sins? You can get in this rut. But there is a
freedom that comes with confession.

> *"Confess your trespasses to one another,*
> *and pray for one another, that you may be*
> *healed" (James 5:16)*

That is a verbal confession to one another. If you want to
be healed from trespasses, from committing these sins,
confess them firstly to God. You have to do 1 John 1:9 first
and foremost. But there is also power in confessing to other
people. Quite often a man should go find another man who
is hopefully more mature than he is—that is usually the
good one—or a brother who is very like-minded. The idea
is to go find a mature person to confess to so they can pray
for you. Confide in someone or a small group of people.

John is going to continue writing. He is writing to us so that
we may not sin. There is no sin that you are stuck in that
you cannot be freed from. There is no sin that you cannot
be delivered from, especially when we do it in a biblical
manner and do what the Bible says.

And then he says, 'And if anyone sins'—if the expectation
was that you would never sin, then writing this would be
foolishness. 'If anyone sins, we have an Advocate with the
Father, Jesus Christ the righteous.'

The Courtroom Setting

From here and into the next verse, John moves into a
courtroom setting. He is going to be using essentially legal
terms. The word 'an Advocate' there is *paraklētos*
(παράκλητος). That is the word in John's Gospel, chapters
14, 15, and 16, where Jesus says, 'I am going to send a
Helper.' It is good that I leave because I am going to send
another Helper, and He is going to be there, and He is

going to declare things to you and bring things to remembrance. That word for Helper there is *paraklētos*. And here now Jesus—so the Holy Spirit and Jesus both receive this title as an Advocate or a Helper.

But in a legal setting, in an ancient Roman or Greek setting, this was specifically used of someone who would be a friend or someone who would come up and testify of your character. We have character testimonies, and this is what a *paraklētos* would do. They would come and speak on your behalf: 'I know what it looks like, but trust me, this person is trustworthy and has been faithful all these years and has done all these good things.' Someone comes in who knows you and talks on your behalf. Jesus is our lawyer.

From Genesis to Revelation, the Bible uses a lot of legal courtroom-like settings, scenarios, and things. We see it in Zechariah, where there is the high priest before the Lord. He is in the courtroom, and there is the prosecuting attorney, Satan, who is bringing accusations. And there is the angel of the Lord, his advocate. Jesus Christ is our lawyer and our advocate.

The opposite of the advocate is the adversary, and that is a name for Satan.

> *"Be sober, be vigilant; because your adversary the devil walks about like a roaring lion, seeking whom he may devour"* *(1 Pet. 5:8)*

> *"Then I heard a loud voice saying in heaven, 'Now salvation, and strength, and the kingdom of our God, and the power of His Christ have come, for the accuser of our brethren, who accused them before our God day and night, has been cast down'"* *(Rev. 12:10)*

23

Again and again, the Bible pictures this courtroom setting—in Revelation, Zechariah, 1 John, and elsewhere—where you have the Father on the throne. You have us, the guilty party. You have a prosecuting attorney, who is Satan, continually bringing accusations. And you have Jesus Christ the righteous, our Advocate, our lawyer, defending us.

Jesus is the greatest lawyer ever. He has never lost a case. No case has ever been won without His counsel. But He only ever represents sinners. It is like you have got this hotshot lawyer, and as long as you get this lawyer, you know you are going to be let free. But before he will take your case, he just wants to know: Did you do it? And if you lie to him, he will not take your case. But if you confess, 'Yeah, I did it. I am guilty,' the lawyer says, 'Okay, do not worry. I have got this.'

And there your lawyer goes up before the judge, and he goes, 'Hey, Dad. Listen, I know this kid is a numskull, but we have got a deal worked out.' Now, we have a problem, though, because no matter how much the judge loves the lawyer, the judge is righteous and there is a law, and the law has been broken, and so there is a fine.

> *"And He Himself is the propitiation for our sins, and not for ours only but also for the whole world" (1 John 2:2)*

He himself, the lawyer, our Advocate Jesus Christ, is the propitiation for our sins. 'Propitiation'—this is the Greek word *hilasmos* (ἱλασμός), an appeasing or a propitiation. Where this word was used a lot in ancient culture and literature was in reference to pagan sacrifices used to appease an angry god. You see, the bad gods were angry, so you would bring the sacrifice to make the volcano go away. But that is the idea—something needs to be paid to appease what has gone on.

In the legal sense, which is the theme in these verses, it is the paying of a fine. A fine has to be paid. And so Jesus says, 'I know I am defending this guy. He is a numskull, but I am going to pay the fine.' And so He steps in in our place and pays that fine so that we do not have to.

It is just a beautiful scene here. We have an Advocate. Jesus is on our side. He is fighting for us. He is interceding on our behalf. He is the mediator between God and man. And we have got an adversary too. We need to remember that Satan is against us. He is trying to stumble us. He is trying to foul us up. He is trying to get us to fall back into sin.

Once Satan can keep someone away from the faith, he will do his best. But once they are in, he will just do his best to make it the most miserable faith. He will make it the most fruitless faith. He will try and rob them of their joy and rob them of all the blessings that they can have.

A great read—or if you do not find the time to read, a great listen—is *The Screwtape Letters* by C.S. Lewis. The whole story is a fictional account about a veteran demon writing letters to his novice nephew. He is writing these letters and giving him advice, and that nephew has got a man that he is supposed to be assigned to. He is giving advice on how to keep him down. But then the man becomes a believer, so then he has to shift gears and give his nephew all this other advice.

You listen to this stuff, and it gives you a glimpse into demonic warfare and the sneakiness and the trickery of the devil. One of my favorite parts is simply where the veteran demon says, 'You know, you can tell that he is being tempted by God. And you might be thinking, I need to come in there and do something dramatic to stop him from becoming a Christian. But let me tell you the best advice, dear nephew: You do not need to do something dramatic. Just distract him, because that works. Just get him thinking about something else. And you can just quickly distract someone from what would have been a great moment, what could have been a turning point in their life. Just put one of the everyday life distractions and anxieties, the cares of this world, and he will not go any further.'

If you like to listen, you can go on YouTube and listen for free. The version I listened to was read by John Cleese, and that was just fun. He does a great job.

For the Whole World

Now, one last part of the verse, but an important part: 'He is the propitiation for our sins, and not for ours only, but also for the whole world.' That is a very highlightable and underlinable verse right there. Jesus Christ paid for our sins, not for ours only, but also for the whole world.

This is not a lone verse.

> *"For God so loved the world that He gave His only begotten Son, that whoever believes in Him should not perish but have everlasting life" (John 3:16)*

The Bible is full of open offers to all to come to know Him and repeated verses that He died for all.

> *"And I, if I am lifted up from the earth, will draw all peoples to Myself" (John 12:32)*

> *"And He died for all, that those who live should live no longer for themselves, but for*

Him who died for them and rose again" (2 Cor. 5:15)

"But we see Jesus, who was made a little lower than the angels, for the suffering of death crowned with glory and honor, that He, by the grace of God, might taste death for everyone" (Heb. 2:9)

"For there is one God and one Mediator between God and men, the Man Christ Jesus, who gave Himself a ransom for all" (1 Tim. 2:5-6)

Do you really mean all? Does all really mean all? Well, one of the greatest verses to nail that down is actually 2 Peter 2:1. My assisting pastor was actually the first one to point this out to me.

"But there were also false prophets among the people, even as there will be false teachers among you, who will secretly bring in destructive heresies, even denying the Lord who bought them, and bring on themselves swift destruction" (2 Pet. 2:1)

The false teachers of 2 Peter are very clearly denounced as heretics, denounced as unbelievers, and they are sentenced to hell. Peter is super clear about where these guys are headed. But he also says these guys denied Jesus, and He is the one who bought them. He paid for their entrance into heaven, and they rejected it.

He is not only the payment for our sins but also the payment for the whole world. And that is a message that we ought to declare. But it is hard to sell something when it seems like the people are not actually sold themselves on it. You might remember those old commercials: 'I am not just the owner; I am a user.' The idea is that as we want to win

27

people to Jesus, we do not want to just be owners. We want to be users. We want to have a faith that other people want to have. We want to have joy unspeakable so that other people would want to have that joy.

The idea is that we want to work out these things in our lives that are hindering us, that are dragging us down, that are stealing our joy, because we want to have that. There is a quote I hear often and love: The perfecting of our faith is not the perfection of performance but the perfection of a relationship.

That is an underlying theme in all we have talked about. It is not about God trying to get you to perform better—'I need to do better; I need to sin less.' Maybe some of that is involved, but that is getting the cart before the horse. That is thinking things backwards. All you need to be thinking about is that you need to have a living and powerful relationship with Jesus Christ, your Savior. And if you are doing anything that is hurting your relationship, you just want the Lord to reveal that to you. You want Him to show that to you so that you can see it. You want to see it how He sees it so that you can confess and say the same thing: 'Yeah, that is ugly sin. That is wretched sin. That is the only kind of sin there is. And Lord, if You think it is disgusting, I want You to make me think it is disgusting. If You think it is horrible, I do not want to think it is little or excusable. No, Lord, I want You to make me think it is as wicked as You think it is, because I want to be near to You. I want to walk in the light as You are in the light. I want to have fellowship with You because I want nothing, not even as small as a grain of sand, to keep me from You. I want to perfect our relationship.'

This is a good ending point for this portion of First John.

Knowing Him
1 John 2:3-11

Keeping His Commandments

John continues his emphasis on authentic faith by connecting knowledge of God with obedience. In verse 3, he writes:

> *"Now by this we know that we know Him, if we keep His commandments." (1 John 2:3)*

This theme of keeping His commandments has been present since the beginning. Jesus Himself declared in John 14:15, "If you love Me, keep My commandments." The concept appears again and again throughout His teaching. Understanding the meaning of the word translated "commandments" is important, as small misunderstandings can turn into large mistakes and false teachings.

The word here is *entolē* (ἐντολή), meaning an order, command, charge, precept, injunction, or commandment. While almost every Bible translation rightfully uses "commandments," it is worth noting that this word does not necessarily refer to *the* commandments in the sense of the Law of Moses. The presence or absence of the article "the" makes a significant difference. When Scripture speaks of "the law," it refers specifically to the Law of Moses. But when it speaks of "law" without the article, it can refer to various principles or laws, such as the law of sin and death.

The term *entolē* simply means any precept, any charge, any injunction—in other words, any teaching from Jesus which believers are expected to follow. In verse 5, John uses "keeping the Word" synonymously with "keeping His commandments" from verse 4, showing that the commandments are not necessarily formal laws, but the teachings of Jesus in general. Some have mistakenly thought that First John's references to keeping commandments mean believers must keep the Old Testament commandments. But John is not saying that. He is saying His commands—His injunctions—the things Jesus taught. Christians who know Jesus do the things He told them to do. That is simply a general principle that believers understand and accept.

Verse 4 states the contrast plainly:

> *"He who says, 'I know Him,' and does not*
> *keep His commandments, is a liar, and the*
> *truth is not in him." (1 John 2:4)*

There are many people today who claim to know God and identify as Christians, yet their lives tell a different story. A telltale, almost definite sign of an unbeliever is when someone begins to explain why they do not need to keep the commands of the Bible. There are babes in Christ who are confused, and God is still working things out in them. But quite often, when someone says, "I'm a Christian, but I don't know about this, this, and this"—explaining why they know better than the Bible—it raises serious questions about the reality of their conversion.

Verse 5 provides the positive side:

> *"But whoever keeps His word, truly the love*
> *of God is perfected in him. By this we know*
> *that we are in Him." (1 John 2:5)*

The idea here is that if a person is keeping His word, the love of God is being perfected in that person. Believers learn that they do not need to keep His commandments harder, better, stronger, and longer in order to be approved.

Rather, those who love God—those whom God loves and accepts—will be found obeying more and more. Obedience is a byproduct of love for God, not the means of earning His approval.

Walking as Jesus Walked

"He who says he abides in Him ought himself also to walk just as He walked."
(1 John 2:6)

This verse goes beyond simply obeying His commands and obeying the things He taught. It speaks to being like Jesus—that believers should be like Jesus. This principle led to the very popular question: What would Jesus do? That really is a great question, because believers need to remember that when Peter tells us that Scripture has given us all things that pertain to life and godliness, we have everything needed to make the right choices on how to live this life (2 Pet. 1:3).

However, the Bible has not given a direct command for every single situation believers face. There is not a direct teaching on every single thing life puts before us. But what can be done is to look to Jesus. Believers can also look to Paul, Peter, and John, because Paul says, "Imitate me, as I also imitate Christ" (1 Cor. 11:1). As Paul looked to Jesus, we see how it lived out in his life. Looking to Jesus enables believers to make decisions that seem befitting of Jesus— understanding how Jesus would handle a given situation.

The Wide Spectrum of Christ's Example

A study of Jesus' interactions throughout the Gospels reveals that there are often disagreements on how Jesus would have handled a situation. Some emphasize that Jesus

31

was the friend of sinners, while others point to His confrontational moments. Everyone tends to have their go-to verses that they jump to. So it is a great reminder that Jesus had some very dramatically different behaviors in different scenarios. The way He handled one situation was nothing like the way He handled another situation.

Right from the start, believers need to understand that forgiving the people nailing you to the cross is on the table, and flipping over tables is also on the table. There is this wide spectrum of appropriate ways to handle a situation, but it is hard because we are not Jesus. We do not have perfect knowledge. We do not have perfect foreknowledge. He knew men's hearts, so He already knew what was going on inside. We do not know men's hearts. Through conversation, we can reveal a little bit about what is going on in there, but He went into situations already knowing. Secondly, He knew how people would respond to every single different kind of probe or stimulus.

There are some people who need to be handled very gently. If you are not gentle with them, they will just break down and fall apart. So you handle them one way. Then there are other kinds of people—and this takes time to learn—where you just have to tell them what it is plainly and directly until they finally get in shape and do what they are supposed to be doing. Everyone has their own ways, and you learn that different people need to be treated differently.

Examples from Jesus' Ministry

Consider a few examples of how Jesus walked. He flipped over the tables—and He did it twice. He did it at His first time at the temple and His last time at the temple in His earthly ministry, as recorded in John and in the other

Gospels. John's account is where He makes the whip (John 2:13-17).

In Matthew 23, in the context of religious hypocrites, one highlighted verse stands out. Matthew 23:15 states:

> *"Woe to you, scribes and Pharisees,*
> *hypocrites! For you travel land and sea to*
> *win one proselyte, and when he is won, you*
> *make him twice as much a son of hell as*
> *yourselves." (Matt. 23:15)*

This is on the table of what would Jesus do. So it is a good reminder for some, because some people forget. Especially people who have never read the Bible—these verses shock them. They did not realize Jesus spoke so straightforwardly about hell.

But then the spectrum flips, and yes, He was also the friend of sinners. The woman caught in adultery was deserving of death. Those famous words are recorded in John 8:7:

> *"He who is without sin among you, let him*
> *throw a stone at her first." (John 8:7)*

But it is also worth noting in that passage that in verse 11, He says, "Who are your accusers?" She says, "No one, Lord." So He says, "Neither do I condemn you; go and sin no more" (John 8:11). It is not like He left her sin unaddressed and untouched.

Jesus and the Sinners

This realization led to further study. When people talk about Jesus the friend of sinners, they sometimes say, "We have to be really gentle and really caring because Jesus was a friend of sinners and loving toward sinners." Upon going through the Gospels again, examining how often Jesus

33

interacted with sinners and how often there are actual details, only one story could really be found out of all the Gospels where Jesus interacted with a sinner, and it was not a sinner coming to Him already repentant, seeking Him out, wanting Jesus to help them and transform them.

There were all these people—they were sinners, they had issues, they had problems—and the religious people would not even minister to them because they were sinners. That was the hypocrisy that Jesus hated. But when these people came to Him, they were repentant and ready to obey Jesus and whatever He said. So sometimes when discussing dealing with sinners, it must be remembered that most of these encounters with Jesus involved people already seeking Him and wanting Him to give them direction and guidance.

The one story that is different is John 4—the woman at the well. This is the one encounter where Jesus engages an unbeliever in a conversation and then quickly turns the conversation from a normal everyday thing—"I need some water, you have water, let's get some water"—into a spiritual conversation about living water. As soon as that spiritual conversation gets going and it seems like she is interested in talking about spiritual things, He immediately addresses her sin issues: "You are right; you have no husband, for the one you are living with now is not your husband, and the four you had before" (John 4:17-18). He does not dodge around the issue. He brings it right to the surface.

The problem is that once again, He had perfect knowledge. He knew where her heart was. He knew how she would respond. It is safe to say that in any situation, believers should be more tactful than Jesus appeared to be, because there needs to be a bit of a buffer zone of safety. We will not go too hard this way, and we will not go too hard that way, because we realize that Jesus had better knowledge. But in that situation, He dealt with her sin.

In the next chapter, John 5, there is the man at the pool of Bethesda. He approaches the man—that is the only other story where Jesus approaches a person who was not already seeking Him. "Do you want to be made well? Rise, take up your bed and walk" (John 5:6, 8). More happens, and then: "Go and sin no more, lest a worse thing come upon you" (John 5:14).

Walking in the Spirit

It is a good note that how did Jesus walk? He was a friend of sinners, but He always brought up sin. He never left things just lingering around in limbo. He made it very clear where He stood on things. He was loving and tactful, but He was always forward. What is found when studying how to walk like Jesus walked is that there is no other answer than this: He walked in the Spirit. He walked being led by the Holy Spirit, full of the Holy Spirit, allowing the Holy Spirit to guide His every step, every thought, every word.

If believers want to walk as Jesus walked, they cannot just cling to the "Woe to you, Pharisees" chapter. They cannot cling to "He who is without sin, cast the first stone" or the "Judge not" words of Jesus. Believers need to be clinging to the Holy Spirit to guide everything they do, so that they are not too far on either end of the spectrum. In fact, really all of us, in any given moment, are in one of three places: either perfect like Jesus (and no one qualifies for that), a little bit too lenient or too gracious (though it sounds hard to say "too gracious," you understand the point), or maybe a little bit too heavy, too hard. We are always going to be either perfect like Jesus, or leaning a little one way or the other. And it is okay to lean a little one way or the other.

That is why being tactful is important—staying a little away from those outer extremes and trying to keep that balance, handling each situation appropriately.

Those who say they abide in Him ought to walk just as He walked. Believers need to be taking everything moment by moment, bringing it before the Lord and asking the Holy Spirit to guide their words so that they can be effective at ministering to people.

The Old and New Commandment

> *"Brethren, I write no new commandment to you, but an old commandment which you have had from the beginning. The old commandment is the word which you heard from the beginning. Again, a new commandment I write to you, which thing is true in Him and in you, because the darkness is passing away, and the true light is already shining." (1 John 2:7-8)*

What John is saying becomes very clear once you get past what initially seems unclear. He is saying, "Listen, these false teachers are bringing new stuff. They are saying, 'I know you have heard the good old gospel, but let me tell you about this new stuff you have never heard about— these deeper teachings the rest of the church does not get, but we get it.' They are coming and bringing these false teachings and challenges." John responds, "No, I am going to be teaching the same good old gospel you have heard from the beginning."

What he is building into will become a major theme of the rest of the book. Up until this point, he has not emphasized the "loving one another" emphasis. Love is one of the key things of this short book, and he is going to be introducing

it here. He is saying it is the same message they have heard:
Love one another. From forty-plus years ago, when Paul
brought the gospel to Asia Minor (modern-day Turkey,
where this is taking place), they heard the message from
Paul to love one another. John is saying, "I am not bringing
you anything new. It is the same message you have always
heard from the beginning."

Verse 8 begins with "again," which is the Greek word *palin*
(πάλιν). This word is most commonly translated "again,"
but it also can mean "on the other hand." In this verse, "on
the other hand" makes sense, because in John 13:34, Jesus
Himself said:

> *"A new commandment I give to you, that
> you love one another; as I have loved you,
> that you also love one another." (John
> 13:34)*

Jesus called it a new commandment. So John is saying,
"Well, on the other hand, it is a new commandment—new
in that Christ said it was a new commandment when He
gave it. This is the new commandment. So it is not a new
commandment in that it is the same one you have heard
your entire walk with Christ. But it is the new
commandment." This removes the paradox of John
seemingly saying two opposite things in verses 7 and 8.

The message is to love one another. Love one another.
Love one another. John will go to the grave continually
saying, "Little children, love one another." This is because,
as verse 8 continues, "the darkness is passing away, and the
true light is already shining."

Light and Darkness

John is talking about the darkness of this age and the light of the age to come. These were terms and phrases often used in that time. The Jewish people also used these phrases—"this age" and "the age to come"—the age they were in and the age that was coming. Ephesians 1:21 speaks of not only "in this age" but also "in that which is to come." There is this age and an age to come. Ephesians 6:12 states:

> *"For we do not wrestle against flesh and blood, but against principalities, against powers, against the rulers of the darkness of this age." (Eph. 6:12)*

This age we live in is known by its darkness. There is darkness in this age, this world being under the power of Satan. But notice how John phrases it: there is darkness in this age, but it is passing away. And the true light which is coming is already starting to shine. As believers love one another and the love of Christ is manifested within them and abounds among them, they begin to see that light grow and grow.

Verse 9 states:

> *"He who says he is in the light, and hates his brother, is in darkness until now." (1 John 2:9)*

John says the same thing in many different ways. You walk in the light or you walk in darkness. You cannot say you love God but disobey His commandments. You cannot say you love God but hate your brother. You cannot say you love God but—and he continues with these contrasts. Verse 10 states:

*"He who loves his brother abides in the
light, and there is no cause for stumbling in
him." (1 John 2:10)*

Verse 11 continues:

*"But he who hates his brother is in darkness
and walks in darkness, and does not know
where he is going, because the darkness has
blinded his eyes." (1 John 2:11)*

Stumbling in Darkness

"There is no cause for stumbling in him"—that verse can
seem puzzling at first. The idea is that there is no stumbling
block to the one who is not in darkness. He is painting a
simple picture. If you are in the light and paying even
halfway attention to what you are doing, you could place a
small box—a block which you might stumble on, a
stumbling block—in the walkway. People walking through,
if the lights are on, are probably not going to fall over the
block because they can see it. They are in the light. But if
all the lights are turned off and someone goes walking, they
might stumble on the block. These people who hate their
brothers are unbelievers who walk in darkness. They
stumble all the time because they are in darkness.

Hateful people are lost and do not know where they are
going. Believers need to remember that. When considering
all the commands in Romans 12—the whole latter portion
full of them—the Sermon on the Mount in chapter 5, and
other places where commands are given to love those who
hate us, bless those who persecute us, pray for those who
spitefully use us (Matt. 5:44), bless and do not curse, do not
repay evil for evil (Rom. 12:14, 17)—all these verses
present challenges.

These commands are hard to do, because it is hard to be nice to mean people. It is hard to want to bless mean jerks. Someone cuts you off in traffic and flips you off, and it is hard to respond with "Bless you." It is just not natural. It is not what the flesh wants to do.

I still remember one of the worst road rage incidents I had a while ago. It was at that light off the freeway in Prosser as you are going into town, where the two lanes merge into one lane. I was just in the right lane—that is just where I was. I had merged left, and we took off. The guy pulled ahead, so I was just right behind him. The guy behind me had to be four car lengths back, and I was just moving at 35 miles an hour or whatever. The guy behind me zipped forward to get side by side with me and then held position. I literally started going into the gravel because I was just ready to cruise over, and this guy was right there. I thought, "Man, you have made it on my prayer list." I was mad at the guy.

But the reality is this: Even with Christians, when a Christian is rude to you or hurts you, is it because they are happy and full of joy? No. It is usually because something is hurting them, something is upsetting them, something is bothering them, to which they are not acting as a Christian ought to act. All the more with an unbeliever—when unbelievers are mean to you, there is a reason for that. It is because they are in darkness. They are blind and prone to stumble in every way, and they are hellbound.

It is easier to pray for them when we realize that these poor people are bound and entrapped by sin. Everyone from a terrorist who is persecuting Christians in these persecuted countries, to people on TV in our own country who are crazy, to those who say and do unbelievable things these days—we need to remember they are blind. They cannot see. They are prone to stumble and do all these stumbling things because they are in darkness. So we can pray for them that they come to the light. Just reminding ourselves of that truth is helpful: the only reason they act that way is because they are hellbound sinners in darkness headed to outer darkness. We can pray for them.

> It is not the same kind of blessing given to fellow believers, but there is a kind of blessing available for them. "Lord, I pray for them that You would bless them by bringing them out of the darkness into the light." It is not just a generic blessing—"I will bless you for that"—but rather, "Lord, bless them by getting them out of that." These people who are in darkness are not believers. It should be obvious to all. If they were believers, they would walk in the light.

> John knows that encouragement alone is not enough. Having strengthened the believer with assurance, he now warns of the one thing that most often erodes it—misdirected love.

The Epistles of John

What Do You Love?
1 John 2:12-17

A Word of Encouragement

This passage begins the first of two brief digressions in John's epistle. Most commentators note that John purposefully steps aside from his main theme in these sections—1 John 2:12-14 and 2:15-17. Throughout the letter, John has been relentlessly warning believers about false teachers, laying out test after test by which one can know whether they are truly in the faith. He has declared that walking in the light distinguishes believers from those in darkness, that keeping His commandments proves genuine love for God, and that loving one's brother is evidence of true faith. John repeats these truths in various ways to make one point clear: believers should be expected to live one way, and unbelievers another. False teachers can be identified by their manner of life. Why listen to those who are not living as they should?

Yet some of what John says is heavy-hitting. In verses 12-14, he pauses to give a word of encouragement.

Little Children, Fathers, and Young Men

> *"I write to you, little children, because your sins are forgiven you for His name's sake. I write to you, fathers, because you have known Him who is from the beginning. I write to you, young men, because you have overcome the wicked one. I write to you, little children, because you have known the Father. I have written to you, fathers,*

> *because you have known Him who is from*
> *the beginning. I have written to you, young*
> *men, because you are strong, and the word*
> *of God abides in you, and you have*
> *overcome the wicked one." (1 John 2:12-14)*

John addresses three groups twice each: little children, fathers, and young men. These appear to be spiritual categories rather than literal age groups. In the Roman world, young men was a specific term referring to men from their late teens or early twenties—when they could marry—through their forties. This was considered the prime of life: getting married, having children, building a family, finding a career. Fathers were men fading from prominence, handing off the torch after having done their part. Little children were those not yet grown, still immature.

John uses two different Greek words for little children and shifts between "I write to you" and "I have written to you." These variations need not be read with great significance. John employs different words throughout the book to paint the same truth from slightly different angles, ensuring his message is heard clearly.

To the little children—those who are babes in the faith—he offers a simple reminder: their sins are forgiven for His name's sake. Satan may come to sow seeds of doubt or confusion, but they need only remember this foundational truth. If they have been forgiven, they are forgiven.

To the fathers, John writes that they have known Him who is from the beginning. He will repeat this exact phrase to them again. For those who are veterans in the faith, it seems they simply need to be reminded of what the main thing is: knowing God, having a relationship with God. Paul writes in Philippians 3 that he counts all things loss for the excellence of the knowledge of Christ Jesus his Lord, that he may know Him, the power of His resurrection, and the fellowship of His sufferings. Knowing God is what it is all about.

To the young men, John says they have overcome the wicked one. This is something young men in particular need to hear—that in the midst of facing battles where they sometimes feel they are losing, they need to remember the wicked one is trying to take them down, but they already have victory in Jesus. They have already overcome.

John then returns to the little children at the end of verse 13: they have known the Father. Remarkably, this is the same truth he gave to the fathers. He is telling these babes in the faith that they possess the same thing the veterans have. They may think they are just getting started, that they do not know anything or what they are doing, but John assures them: they are forgiven, and they know the same God the mature believers know. They are in the same position. They need not think less of themselves.

To the fathers, he repeats himself exactly: they have known Him who is from the beginning. For those seasoned in the faith, the reminder is simply this—the main thing is the main thing. Knowing God and having a relationship with Him is what matters most.

Finally, to the young men again, John adds to his earlier encouragement. He says they are strong, the word of God abides in them, and they have overcome the wicked one. After some of the heavy-hitting truths presented earlier, people might doubt themselves. Perhaps they wonder if they are truly walking in the light as He is in the light. John reassures them: these are general principles to help distinguish unbelievers from believers. Do not start picking apart your walk and doubting your salvation. You are strong. The word of God is in you. This is encouragement.

It is worth noting that all the main verbs in these verses are in the Greek perfect tense, which indicates things that have been done and remain in effect—a present consequence of a past event. When someone becomes saved, they are immediately in the Father and in the Son. Their sins are forgiven. They have overcome the wicked one. These are accomplished realities, settled matters that need not be worried over.

The Call to Transformation

> *Do not love the world or the things in the world. If anyone loves the world, the love of the Father is not in him." (1 John 2:15)*

From this word of encouragement, John moves directly into a word of exhortation and warning in verse 15: do not love the world. This brings to mind another crucial text in Romans 12, a passage that addresses the same tension between transformation and conformity.

> *"I beseech you therefore, brethren, by the mercies of God, that you present your bodies a living sacrifice, holy, acceptable to God, which is your reasonable service." (Rom. 12:1)*

Consider an illustration. If a stranger approached and offered to pay off your mortgage, your car loan, all your credit card bills, and then deposited twenty thousand dollars into your bank account—and after completing all this at the bank, turned to you and asked if you could spare a dollar for the Coke machine—would you hesitate? Of course not. It would seem entirely reasonable to give a dollar after receiving such overwhelming generosity.

This is Paul's point in Romans 12:1. When Christians realize what God has done for them—that He gave His Son—it is reasonable to present our bodies as living sacrifices. This is simply another way of saying, "God, You can have my whole life. You can have all of me. Everything. Take it. It is Yours." If believers genuinely desire to do that, then verse 2 comes into play.

> *"And do not be conformed to this world, but*
> *be transformed by the renewing of your*
> *mind, that you may prove what is that good*
> *and acceptable and perfect will of God."*
> *(Rom. 12:2)*

God wants to show the world His glory, His love, His mercy, His awesomeness through believers. He wants the world to see His good and acceptable and perfect will, and He does this by proving it through His people. The word translated prove was commonly used when testing gold to determine its quality. God says He wants to show the world who He is through the tests and trials believers face. To do this, believers must choose one of two roads: do not be conformed to this world, but be transformed.

The Greek word for transform is *metamorphosis*—the same process butterflies undergo. A caterpillar builds a cocoon, its body literally melts into a formless substance, and then it rebuilds itself into a butterfly. This is how God wants to work in believers. He wants to transform them. The world wants to conform them. Conforming involves beating something into a certain shape—forcing it into a mold. The world is beating on believers through countless influences, trying to conform them into its image. God is trying to transform believers into His image by the renewing of their

47

minds. The word of God does a work within, renewing minds. Believers come to church and get their minds washed—cleansed and renewed. This is the reality: minds need to be washed, renewed, and cleansed.

Do Not Love the World

John provides further instruction on how not to be conformed to this world. In verse 15, he writes, "Do not love the world or the things in the world. If anyone loves the world, the love of the Father is not in him."

This is not a new teaching, nor is it unique to John. Jesus said in the Sermon on the Mount:

> *"No one can serve two masters; for either he will hate the one and love the other, or else he will be loyal to the one and despise the other. You cannot serve God and mammon." (Matt. 6:24)*

Many translations render this as "God and money," but the word is literally mammon. Mammon was a god—the god of possessions, with money being the primary focus. Jesus is saying a choice must be made. One god will be worshiped, and the other will not receive the attention it ought to have.

James, the half-brother of Jesus, writes in James 4:4:

> *"Adulterers and adulteresses! Do you not know that friendship with the world is enmity with God? Whoever therefore wants to be a friend of the world makes himself an enemy of God."*

These passages all deal with "the world," but it is important to understand what is meant by this term, as words can have different meanings depending on context.

The world can refer to creation. God made the world—the trees, the birds, the oceans—all part of this physical creation. There is nothing wrong with loving that. It is part of God's creation, and when He created it, He said it was all good.

The world can also mean mankind. John 3:16 says, "For God so loved the world that He gave His only begotten Son, that whoever believes in Him should not perish but have everlasting life." It cannot be wrong to love the world in this sense, because God does. He loves mankind. He loves humanity, the people in the world. Loving the world in that way is not wrong.

But here in this text, and most often in the Bible, the phrase the world refers to the world system—all that is going on in this world that is opposed to God. In reality, it is all under the control of the god of this age, the god of this world. These are titles given to the devil in Scripture. Satan holds these names. Certain things were forfeited to him in the Garden of Eden, giving him power and control to do things with this world. Love for this world is incompatible with love for the Father. Believers cannot love this world system. They cannot love the things that have been placed in this world in opposition to God.

The Threefold Enemy

In verse 16, John begins to explain in more detail what constitutes the world:

> *"For all that is in the world—the lust of the flesh, the lust of the eyes, and the pride of*

*life—is not of the Father but is of the
world." (1 John 2:15)*

There is a battle believers fight. Whether they know it or
not, they are part of the fight and face it every day. It has
been said that the Christian's threefold enemy is the world,
the flesh, and the devil. While the focus here is on the
world, it is important to understand that these three work in
tandem. They work together as a team. James references
this in James 3:15, speaking of ungodly wisdom:

*"This wisdom does not descend from above,
but is earthly, sensual, demonic."*

Earthly—of the world. Sensual—of the flesh. Demonic—of
the devil. These three forces—the world, the flesh, and the
devil—work together.

The Fire Triangle

Consider the fire triangle. To make a fire, three elements
are required: air, fuel, and heat. Fires must breathe. Fires
must have something to consume. Fires must have heat to
ignite. Without any one of these three, there is no fire. Fire
extinguishers work by removing one of these elements—
some remove heat by making the fire extremely cold, while
others smother the fire with foam, cutting off the oxygen.
Remove one element, and the fire dies.

As Christians, there is a temptation triangle: the world, the
flesh, and the devil. If any one of the three were removed,
temptations would lose their power.

The Bible speaks of a thousand years when Jesus will rule
and reign on the earth. Revelation tells us that Satan will be
bound for those thousand years. During that time, one part
of the triangle will be gone, and the world will be very
different without Satan here trying to lure people away.

In heaven, there will be no sin. One major reason for this is that believers will receive new bodies. They will no longer have this flesh to deal with—glorified bodies that are no longer fallen, that do not have fleshly desires. When Adam and Eve ate of the fruit, there was a transformation that took place in them. Suddenly they saw and thought in ways they never had before.

The world, however, is something that must be dealt with in this life. Satan uses the world to get at the flesh. He knows he has the ability to attack believers, and he does it through the world. He takes things in the world and uses them as worldly temptations.

The Lust of the Flesh, the Lust of the Eyes, and the Pride of Life

> *"For all that is in the world—the lust of the flesh, the lust of the eyes, and the pride of life—is not of the Father but is of the world." (1 John 2:16)*

The worldly temptations are listed in verse 16 and can be summarized as passions, possessions, and power.

First, there are the passions—the lust of the flesh. To understand this properly, it is important to note that the word *lust* in Greek is much broader than in English. When we use the word lust, it is almost always sexual. But in Greek, it simply means a strong desire or passion. Jesus used this exact Greek word when He said, "I desire strongly to eat this Passover with you" on the night of the Last Supper. It is not necessarily wrong to have a strong desire, but the lust of the flesh is a passion that comes from within and wants to be satisfied.

This is where things like sexual immorality appear. This is where the desire to be gluttonous and eat excessively arises. There are the desires to sleep and rest and do nothing because the body craves checking out and being done. Believers are continually crucifying the flesh because it takes natural desires that God gave and twists them into sinful expressions. It is acceptable to desire food. It is acceptable to desire rest. It is acceptable to desire sex. All of these have appropriate places, times, and ways—and inappropriate ones. But all people have this flesh, and there is a cry from within.

Second, there is the lust of the eyes—the possessions from without. These are the external things seen every day that tempt. This is envy. This is covetousness. This is greed. This is seeing things and wanting them.

Third, there is the pride of life—power or position. People want power. Power might be thought of in a limited sense, but consider it this way: people want to be thought of in a certain way. They want others to think they are smart, attractive, successful. They want status. Much of this is about wanting to be positioned above other people. Satan will determine which area is the weak point for each person, as people might be strong in one and weak in another.

Satan's Timeless Strategy

Satan uses the world to get at the flesh through the lust of the flesh, the lust of the eyes, and the pride of life. He has been using these three moves since the beginning.

In the Garden of Eden, Satan tempted Eve to eat of the fruit. What did he get her to see? That the fruit she was not allowed to eat was good for food—her flesh would be satisfied. It was pleasant to the eyes—her eyes being satisfied. And it was desirable to make one wise—the idea of power, pride, and position. Satan told her she would become like gods. Here in the Garden of Eden, the first time Satan attacks anyone, he uses these three things.

Throughout the Bible, this pattern continues. In Deuteronomy 17, God warns that one day the people will want a king. If they choose a king, he must not be caught up in three things: he cannot multiply horses, multiply wives, or greatly multiply silver and gold for himself.

Multiplying horses must be understood in proper historical context. Most ancient battles did not involve huge armies of horses charging at each other, as depicted in movies. Horses were actually quite rare. Whole nations had no horses, and some had only a few. Not everyone had a sword. In some of the battles with the Philistines recorded in Judges, most of Israel did not have swords or any metal weapons at all. They had wooden implements and farming equipment. This is why the Bible talks about beating plowshares into swords—it was a real thing, because not everyone had proper weapons. For a king, multiplying horses was a way to become a powerful nation. If a king could acquire many horses, he would be nearly undefeatable. But the king was not supposed to strive after power.

He was not supposed to multiply wives—appealing to the lust of his flesh. And he was not supposed to greatly multiply silver and gold for himself. Note the phrase greatly multiply. It is not wrong to have silver and gold, but when a king sets his heart on greatly multiplying it, he no longer possesses wealth—wealth possesses him. There is a significant difference.

The Bible makes it clear in 1 Timothy 6 that the love of money is the root of all evil. It is not the money itself, but the love of it. In that same chapter, Paul gives instructions to rich Christians on how to live. It was not wrong to be rich. It was wrong to set one's heart on wealth to the point where it owns the person rather than the person owning it.

Jesus's Temptation

One final example of these three forces at work in the Bible is Jesus's temptation by Satan, which is perhaps the best illustration. If Satan were to go head-to-head with the Son of God, he would bring out his best. He would not hold back or use halfway measures. He would use the most effective strategies he had.

Jesus had been in the desert, fasting for forty days. After forty days, He was hungry. What did Satan do first? He said, "If You are the Son of God, command these stones to become bread." He was appealing to Jesus's fleshly needs—the lust of the flesh. This was not necessarily sexual; this was physical. The body was crying out for food, and Satan tried to have Jesus acquire it in an ungodly way.

Jesus rebuked him and quoted Scripture. Satan then tried something else. The devil took Him up on a high mountain and showed Him all the kingdoms of the world in a moment of time. In verse 6, Satan said, "All this authority I will give You, and their glory; for this has been delivered to me, and I give it to whomever I wish. Therefore, if You will worship before me, all will be Yours."

The lust of the eyes. It is worth noting that Satan says, "Look at everything in this world—it is mine to give." And Jesus does not tell him he is wrong. Satan does possess this power. He can offer any possession. Nations, kingdoms, anything the eyes desire. But again, Jesus rebuked him and quoted Scripture: "You shall worship the Lord your God, and Him only you shall serve."

Finally, Satan brought Him to Jerusalem, to the highest point of the temple, and said, "If You are the Son of God, throw Yourself down from here." Why? Because, Satan said, the angels will come and catch You. What is the significance? If Jesus did this in a great display with everyone at the temple watching, the angels saving Him, it would let the world know who He is. It would reveal Him as the Son of God, and everyone would recognize and worship Him. This is the pride of life—appealing to pride. People would finally recognize You as they ought to.

Three times Satan tempted Jesus, and he used the lust of the eyes, the lust of the flesh, and the pride of life. All three times, Jesus quoted Scripture. This is significant because Jesus is the Son of God and could have handled Satan in many different ways, but He chose to do it in the same way believers can do it.

Peter writes in 1 Peter 5 that if believers resist the devil, he will flee from them. How is this done? When Satan's temptation comes, it must be tested against Scripture. Find the Scripture that says, "No, here is why, Satan." Satan did not give up after the first rebuke—he tried again. Jesus gave him Scripture. Satan tried again. Jesus gave him Scripture. Eventually Satan left and waited to return at another opportune time. He was not done with Jesus forever, and he will not be done with believers forever. But this is how to resist the devil so that he will flee.

What Do You Love?

The real question is: how does one know if they are getting caught up in worldly things? How can someone tell if they are struggling with the lust of the flesh, the lust of the eyes, or the pride of life? The first and simplest way to examine this is to ask a question: What do you love?

Two Greek Words for Love

This becomes a fruitful area of study when considering that there is more than one Greek word for love. When reading the New Testament, a Greek document translated into English, it becomes apparent that the Greeks had four different words for love. When these are translated into English, the result is often love, love, love, love—making distinctions difficult to see.

The two most common and important to understand are agapē and phileō love.

The Greek word *phileō* speaks of fondness and affection. It is typically translated as brotherly love. The city of Philadelphia combines *phileō* (love) and *adelphos* (brothers)—the city of brotherly love. It is a fondness, a liking of something, a strong affection for it.

In contrast, *agapē* is the word typically described as God's love, because this is the love the Bible always speaks of God having. *Agapē* is not a feeling; it is an action. This is a verb—something one does. *Agapē* love always comes at a cost. *Agapē* love always involves sacrifice.

Husbands cannot *agapē* their wives as Christ *agapēd* the church without sacrifice. That is what believers are called to do. The sacrifice does not always mean giving up something of monetary value. Sometimes simply biting one's tongue is a sacrifice. These are sacrifices. *Agapē* love is giving preference to the other, giving them not what they deserve but love instead.

The Command: Do Not Agapē the World

This text is telling believers not to *agapē* the world—not *phileō*. John Stott wrote an insightful observation:

> *"Love is a fit subject for such a commandment and prohibition because it is not an uncontrollable emotion, but the steady devotion of the will."*

This *agapē* word is not merely something one feels; it is a choice. This distinction is freeing in an important way.

The obvious must be stated: *phileō* means fondness, and believers should not have even the smallest bit of fondness for sin. The Bible says that the fear of the Lord is the beginning of wisdom and the beginning of all knowledge, and the fear of the Lord is to hate sin. Believers cannot be fond of sin in any way, shape, or form. That is wrong.

But so much of this world is amoral—it is neither good nor bad. It simply exists. And it is acceptable to be fond of some things. It is acceptable to be fond of sports. It is acceptable to be fond of hunting and fishing. It is acceptable to be fond of cars, clothing, or music. The point is that it is not a command forbidding all enjoyment of anything in this world.

But *agapē* is when it starts coming at a cost. When someone begins sacrificing on behalf of these things, giving up other things for these things, then the line has been crossed from *phileō* love into *agapē* love. Do not *agapē* this world. Love is all about choices.

Love Reveals Itself in Choices

What does someone choose when they have a choice? While there may not be a sinful or righteous answer for a favorite type of cookie, candy, or ice cream, preferences still reveal something. For instance, if presented with a huge platter of cookies but homemade chocolate chip cookies were available, the choice would be clear—because that is the one truly loved. Similarly, carrot cake is preferred above all other cakes, and Butterfingers above all other candy.

Do these silly preferences not show where the heart is? When given a choice, the selection reveals the true desire. This is where the heart really is. The same principle applies to life. What is prioritized in life? People can say their priorities are one thing, but the day-to-day choices they make reveal what their priorities truly are.

One of the obvious indicators is what money is spent on and where time is spent. D.L. Moody said he could tell more about the spirituality of a man from looking at his checkbook than from his prayer book. He realized what Jesus taught: "Where your treasure is, there your heart will be also." People often invest their time and money into the places where their hearts are most tied.

Really, one of the biggest indicators is this: What do you skip or say no to because something else is more important?

An obvious example is found in wedding vows. When someone says yes to their spouse, there is always that piece in the vows that says, "Forsaking all others till death do us part." The idea is that when a commitment is made in one area, all the things that would try to come between that commitment must be refused.

When it comes to loving and serving the Lord, it is necessary to determine what God wants done personally. Then it must be recognized that Satan is going to show up with temptations. He will use all kinds of things in the world to try to prevent the very things God has called believers to do.

A Word About Hobbies and Priorities

This is never meant to be heavy-handed condemnation, because one person's sins always seem uglier than another's. Someone might say, "If you are into sports, you are obviously a worldly sinner. But lifting weights is fine, and working on cars is actually a very admirable thing—because my hobbies are awesome hobbies, and yours are a waste of time, and you ought to be reading your Bible instead."

That is the joke—people can look at other people's choices with judgment. But that is not the point John is making. The point is for each person to look at their own heart and how they have been spending their time, their money, and their thought life. What do you daydream about? Where does your mind go when it has the freedom to think freely? That will begin to reveal what is loved and where the heart truly is.

The solution is not forsaking all these things with legalistic rules—Christians should not do this, Christians should not do that, Christians need to limit themselves to this much time at that. The solution is really falling in love with God, having a knowledge of the Father and of the Son, and growing in that relationship where love for Him dictates actions. Love dictates choices. There is no need to worry about legalistic rules when someone genuinely loves God, and that love changes the way they live.

Pastor Chuck Smith said this in the book Harvest:

"I don't want it ever said that we preach an easy kind of Christian experience at Calvary Chapel. But I also do not want to make the same mistake that the Holiness Church made thirty years ago. Without knowing it, they drove out and lost a whole generation of young people with a negative no-movie, no-dance, no-smoke gospel. Let us at Calvary not be guilty of the same mistake. Instead, let us trust God and emphasize the work of the Holy Spirit within individual lives. It is exciting and much more real and natural to allow the Spirit to dictate change. Let us never be guilty of forcing our Western Christian subculture of clean-shaven, short-hair styles or dress on anyone. We want change to come from inside out. We simply declare that drugs, striving to become a millionaire, or making sports your whole life is not where true fulfillment or ultimate meaning lies. Because the end of all these goals is emptiness and disappointment."

More Is Caught Than Taught

Children are always watching. They can be told what is important, but they will watch what is actually made important far more closely. One thing they will watch is when something said to be important comes into conflict with something loved. Every now and then, those two things will collide, and they will watch and see the response. This will speak volumes.

This is not a legalistic rule that church can never be skipped or that certain activities are always forbidden. The point is that when a decision is made about what the family will do, and the children ask, "But didn't you want to go do that?", the response can be, "We did, but we have priorities in our family, and so we are going to forsake some things we enjoy for the things we know are important." The children will catch that in time. It will stick with them, and they will remember it.

Living in the World, Not of the World

It is important to understand that God never asks believers to leave this world. Jesus prayed in His high priestly prayer:

> *"I do not pray that You should take them out of the world, but that You should keep them from the evil one. They are not of the world, just as I am not of the world. Sanctify them by Your truth. Your word is truth." (John 17:15-17)*

Jesus is praying to the Father that God would protect believers and help them make good choices while they are in the world.

A wrong approach seen in some churches is total withdrawal: no movies, no going out here, no doing this, no doing that. At a certain point, people become so cut off from society that they can no longer be salt and light.

But when serious, devoted Christians are part of sports teams, little leagues, clubs, and other groups in this world, there is opportunity for influence. Years ago, while serving as a pastor in Ellensburg, I resigned from my public job to become a full-time pastor. I missed hanging out with unbelievers because I no longer had regular interaction with them. Last year, I started posting videos of me working on

61

my car. Former students from my auto shop classes and former friends from years past started reaching out and talking again. Suddenly conversations were happening about cars, and those conversations turned into spiritual conversations. Those kinds of conversations were not happening when I was only talking to Christians and hanging out with Christians.

God will use things of this world in great ways as long as they do not own believers and do not become the things that are loved above Him.

Standing Before Christ

It is a sobering reminder that later in this chapter, in verse 28, John writes:

> *"And now, little children, abide in Him, that when He appears, we may have confidence and not be ashamed before Him at His coming."*

Believers must all stand before the judgment seat of Christ and give an account of the things done in the body, whether good or bad. Unbelievers will not be ashamed when they stand before Jesus—they will be terrified. But believers, there will be some who might actually feel they have something to be ashamed of.

A common question I have heard raised is: why are there tears in heaven that need to be wiped away? One possibility is that people stand before Jesus and realize: Why did I waste so much of my life, my time, and my heart on worthless things?

The World Is Passing Away

This ties directly into the final verse of this passage:

> *"And the world is passing away, and the lust of it; but he who does the will of God abides forever." (1 John 2:17)*

Beyond the reality of loving God, there must be a constant awareness that all these things—though it is acceptable to phileō them, to participate in them and be fond of them—are going to pass away. Believers must always remind themselves that these things are temporary.

A personal example illustrates this truth well. One of my favorite hobbies for over twenty years has been exercise. When my wife and I first met, we both were exercise enthusiasts. But people keep telling me that no matter how much I exercise, this body is going to fall apart someday. Slowly, I am seeing it happen little by little. That is the reality. At least in this life, the body is visibly aging. It does not do what it used to do as well as it used to do it. The question becomes: Do you want to keep investing all this time? The answer is yes, but with perspective—realizing it is simply enjoyed while also listening to sermons, worship music, and inviting people over for fellowship. The hobby is made edifying. But there is also the awareness that this whole body is going to burn. Too much heart cannot be put into it, but it can be enjoyed to some degree.

That is the reality: this world is passing away.

As a pastor, funerals are part of ministry. People come up and share memories of the deceased. Never once has anyone come up and said things like, "He had the coolest car," or "Remember all the medals he accumulated?" or "That guy had so much money. Do you remember the money he had?" People talk about character. They talk about who the person was. They think about the legacy left behind. If the only legacy someone leaves can be sorted out in a will, they have left their children nothing.

This world is passing away. As long as that truth is remembered, and as long as God is checking the heart, good decisions will be made.

Charles Spurgeon said, "Unless we purposely live with the view of the next world, we cannot make much out of our present existence."

George Mueller said, "The longer I live, the more I am enabled to realize that I have but one life to live on earth and that this one life is but a brief life for sowing in comparison with eternity for reaping." He understood that choices made during this short life will be experienced in their results forever in eternity.

Only One Life

To close, here are a few verses from C.T. Studd's poem "Only One Life." C.T. Studd was a professional athlete who left sports and went to the mission field.

> *"Two little lines I heard one day,*
> *Traveling along life's busy way;*
> *Bringing conviction to my heart,*
> *And from my mind would not depart;*
> *Only one life, 'twill soon be past,*
> *Only what's done for Christ will last.*
>
> *Only one life, yes only one,*
> *Soon will its fleeting hours be done;*
> *Then, in 'that day' my Lord to meet,*
> *And stand before His Judgment seat;*
> *Only one life, 'twill soon be past,*

Only what's done for Christ will last.

Oh let my love with fervor burn,
And from the world now let me turn;
Living for Thee, and Thee alone,
Bringing Thee pleasure on Thy throne;
Only one life, 'twill soon be past,
Only what's done for Christ will last.

Only one life, yes only one,
Now let me say, 'Thy will be done';
And when at last I'll hear the call,
I know I'll say 'twas worth it all';
Only one life, 'twill soon be past,
Only what's done for Christ will last."

Conclusion

The desire is not to lay heavy burdens from the pulpit or to make people feel that their hobbies are wrong or that they cannot do certain things. But the desire is for the church to be sober-minded, thinking about how time is spent, what is done, and recognizing belief in a life after this one that will go on for eternity. The things done here are going to make a difference there. When this earth is left behind, the hope is that a lasting difference has been made for eternity.

John's warning is clear: do not love the world or the things in the world. The world is passing away, and the lust of it. But he who does the will of God abides forever. Believers must guard their hearts, examine what they love, and ensure that their affections are set on things above, not on things on the earth. The call is to fall so deeply in love with God that all else fades in comparison—not through legalistic restrictions, but through genuine devotion that transforms how life is lived.

65

The Epistles of John

What do you love? That question deserves honest
examination. The answer will reveal where the heart truly
is and what will remain when all else passes away.

Abiding in Truth
1 John 2:18-29

The Last Hour and Antichrist

Verse 18 moves into a new topic:

> *"Little children, it is the last hour; and as*
> *you have heard that the Antichrist is coming,*
> *even now many antichrists have come, by*
> *which we know that it is the last hour."*
> *(1 John 2:18)*

The Doctrine of Imminency

The phrase "it is the last hour" points to what is called the doctrine of imminency. Throughout the Old Testament, there are references to the last days. In some sense, the last days is actually a term that gets used in different ways. There are the very last days before Christ's coming— literally days and a few years period. But on the day of Pentecost, Peter made reference to it already being the last days. The idea is that there have been these times in history that were leading up to the Christ. And now that He has come, we are in those last days—the last major dispensation before He returns to set up His kingdom.

The last hour is where John is pointing to this idea. John, Peter, Paul—all of them believed in the doctrine of imminency, that there was nothing to wait for before Christ's return. Really, since this time period, there has never been a period where Jesus could not have returned. Some look at things like Israel becoming a nation again as an important sign, but He could have raptured the church before Israel was a nation, and then the Antichrist could have shown up and given them the nation. It did not have to happen first.

What believers are watching is the things unfolding. It seems like eyes are being opened and more and more things are being seen related to His second coming. So it sure looks like it is close now. But the idea of the last hour is that we are in a time period where He could come at any hour. This is why Matthew 24:42 states:

> *"Watch therefore, for you do not know what*
> *hour your Lord is coming." (Matt. 24:42)*

That is what he means by "the last hour"—we are in the last hour because we do not know what hour He is coming. So it could be this hour or the next hour. He is just pointing out the imminency of Christ.

What are they expecting? If you back up two verses prior to this in Matthew 24, it speaks of the rapture:

> *"Then two men will be in the field: one will*
> *be taken and the other left." (Matt. 24:40)*

The doctrine of imminency—that Jesus could come at any time—only really works with a pre-tribulation rapture. There are wonderful believers who have post-tribulation rapture views, believing He comes at the end of the tribulation, or in the middle of the tribulation. But if Jesus comes at the end of the tribulation, there is no need to wait for Jesus because the Antichrist has to come first, and the seal judgments have to come, and all these other things have to happen first. So there is no need to be waiting for Him. It is not the imminency of Jesus; it is the imminency of all these other things.

Another great passage is Luke 17:26-29:

> *"And as it was in the days of Noah, so it will*
> *be also in the days of the Son of Man: They*
> *ate, they drank, they married wives, they*
> *were given in marriage, until the day that*
> *Noah entered the ark, and the flood came*
> *and destroyed them all. Likewise as it was*
> *also in the days of Lot: They ate, they drank,*
> *they bought, they sold, they planted, they*
> *built; but on the day that Lot went out of*
> *Sodom it rained fire and brimstone from*
> *heaven and destroyed them all." (Luke*
> *17:26-29)*

What is it about the days of Noah that Jesus is talking about? They ate, they drank, they married, they were given in marriage. None of that speaks of immorality. That just speaks about life—day-to-day stuff. But then one day, out of nowhere, the flood came and everyone did not see it coming. In the next two verses, He gives a second example to add clarity—just like the days of Lot. They ate, they drank, they bought, they sold, they planted, they built. Again, it has nothing to do with the moral conditions of the world. It is simply saying life was going on. But then, out of nowhere, on the day that Lot went out of Sodom, it rained fire and brimstone from heaven and destroyed them all.

Jesus proceeds in Luke 17 to again say—it is a separate account from Matthew 24, two different sermons—two men are in a field. One will be taken, the other will be left behind. So again, it is this idea that this doctrine of imminency, where life will be going on like normal and He is going to come at an hour that no one knows, only works if the first thing happening is Him coming.

It is also worth noting that at the end of the tribulation, there is no way a believer and an unbeliever are going to be working in the field and sleeping in the bed when believers are running for their lives and unbelievers are getting the mark of the beast. That does not make any sense at all. So if there is any period of time where two will be together, one is taken and one is left, it has to be at a time when believers and unbelievers are still comingling together like normal—husband and wife, two in a bed.

All that said, that is what John is saying: It is the last hour. He believed, and God wanted him to believe, that Jesus could come at any time. God wanted the people in the 1800s and the 1900s to believe Jesus could come at any time. And God wants us to believe that Jesus could come at any time. What imminency rightly does to a real believer with a biblical understanding is it makes us count the cost of what we do. It makes us live in a way where we know that our time is limited. Believers are not escapists—they just fully believe they have limited time and ought to use their time wisely.

The Antichrist

Returning to verse 18, John says, "And as you have heard that the Antichrist is coming, even now many antichrists have come, by which we know that it is the last hour."

The Greek word *anti* is a prefix that can mean "against," but in the Greek it also can mean "instead of." It has a more diverse meaning. So he is pointing out there have been many against Christ—all these people against Christ who have been showing up. It is showing us that things are ramping up here because of these last days. But eventually one will arise who is the instead-of Christ. He will be the replacement Messiah whom the Jews will turn to and worship, and the whole world will turn to him. This is the character whom we call the Antichrist.

In 1 John 2, the word Antichrist with a lowercase 'a' shows up twice. It also shows up in chapter 4 of 1 John, and in 2 John, verse 7. These are the only places the word "antichrist" appears in the Bible. But this man has many other names, and it is worth quickly reviewing those:

> *"Let no one deceive you by any means; for that Day will not come unless the falling away comes first, and the man of sin is revealed, the son of perdition." (2 Thess. 2:3)*

He is called the Man of Sin and the Son of Perdition. The fact that he will be revealed reminds believers that we are not in the tribulation, because the Antichrist will be revealed during that time.

Just a few verses later, he is called the Lawless One:

> *"And then the lawless one will be revealed, whom the Lord will consume with the breath of His mouth and destroy with the brightness of His coming." (2 Thess. 2:8)*

It says again:

> *"The coming of the lawless one is according to the working of Satan, with all power, signs, and lying wonders, and with all unrighteous deception among those who perish, because they did not receive the love of the truth, that they might be saved." (2 Thess. 2:9-10)*

There is concern today because there have always been people—even in the early church, such as the Montanists, an early church group that were like hyper-Pentecostals, way off the reservation on things—who are really caught up in signs and wonders. Believers are biblical Christians who believe in signs and wonders, but they also need to be guarded because the Antichrist is coming with signs and wonders. That is not the main thing. Believers need to be cautious about that.

But there is no need to worry if you love the truth. The people who love the truth are not going to be deceived by these things because they are grounded in the Word. They are going to be protected. But the people who do not love the truth, who are not really into the Bible, will not have that protection from these deceptions.

In the Old Testament, he is called the Little Horn:

> *"I was considering the horns, and there was another horn, a little one, coming up among them, before whom three of the first horns were plucked out by the roots. And there, in this horn, were eyes like the eyes of a man, and a mouth speaking pompous words."*
> *(Dan. 7:8)*

In one of Daniel's visions of the beasts, it starts off with ten horns representing ten nations. Then this little one comes up and seems to take over three of them, and things go on from there.

In Daniel 9, he is called the Prince Who Is to Come:

> *"Know therefore and understand, that from the going forth of the command to restore and build Jerusalem until Messiah the Prince, there shall be seven weeks and sixty-two weeks; the street shall be built again, and the wall, even in troublesome*

*times. And after the sixty-two weeks Messiah
shall be cut off, but not for Himself; and the
people of the prince who is to come shall
destroy the city and the sanctuary. The end
of it shall be with a flood, and till the end of
the war desolations are determined." (Dan.
9:25-26)*

There is this tie between Messiah the Prince versus the
prince who is to come. In the next verse, he is called the
One Who Makes Desolate:

*"Then he shall confirm a covenant with
many for one week; but in the middle of the
week he shall bring an end to sacrifice and
offering. And on the wing of abominations
shall be one who makes desolate, even until
the consummation, which is determined, is
poured out on the desolate." (Dan. 9:27)*

He is coming in on the wings of abominations and he is the
one who makes desolate.

In Daniel 11, he is called the Willful King:

*"Then the king shall do according to his
own will: he shall exalt and magnify himself
above every god, shall speak blasphemies
against the God of gods, and shall prosper
till the wrath has been accomplished; for
what has been determined shall be done."
(Dan. 11:36)*

He has gotten the title Willful King from this passage.

In Zechariah 11, he is referred to as the Idol Shepherd—or more accurately, the Worthless Shepherd:

> *"For indeed I will raise up a shepherd in the*
> *land who will not care for those who are cut*
> *off, nor seek the young, nor heal those that*
> *are broken, nor feed those that still stand.*
> *But he will eat the flesh of the fat and tear*
> *their hooves in pieces. Woe to the worthless*
> *shepherd, who leaves the flock! A sword*
> *shall be against his arm and against his*
> *right eye; his arm shall completely wither,*
> *and his right eye shall be totally blinded."*
> *(Zech. 11:16-17)*

The King James actually calls him the Idol Shepherd, but the word worthless is where we get 'idol' from. This passage describes how he will receive something and his face is going to be distorted and his arm is going to be distorted. At the end of Revelation 13, people are going to be wearing the mark of the beast on their arm and on their face. So there are interesting ties to all these scriptures.

In Revelation 13, he is called the Beast of the Sea:

> *"Then I stood on the sand of the sea. And I*
> *saw a beast rising up out of the sea, having*
> *seven heads and ten horns, and on his horns*
> *ten crowns, and on his heads a blasphemous*
> *name." (Rev. 13:1)*

The second half of Revelation 13 talks about the beast from the land, who is the False Prophet. The beast from the sea is the Antichrist. It talks about how he will receive a mortal wound, but then he will miraculously survive it.

A.W. Pink had a huge long study on the Antichrist, and there are many more verses talking about him. As believers go through the whole Bible, these things pop up again and again. It takes revisiting them again and again to get a flow for it. But once you start seeing the connections, they are hard to unsee. Once you see the material in Zechariah right next to the material in Revelation, it makes sense. These authors are talking about the same person. You get some details from here and a little bit more details from there, and you can bring them together and get a fuller picture of what is going on.

False Teachers Departing

In verse 19, John talks about these false teachers:

> *"They went out from us, but they were not of us; for if they had been of us, they would have continued with us; but they went out that they might be made manifest, that none of them were of us." (1 John 2:19)*

This verse is quoted often because it is helpful. It is confusing when people leave the church. When people stop attending a healthy church that is recognized as a normal church and either stop going to any kind of gathering at all, or start going or doing something else that is a bit off and different, it raises questions. Often, people who get caught up in false teachings and heresy will leave the church because all those church people have it wrong, and they have it figured out. They will come over here with their three friends who all hold these certain views and just do their thing.

It is tough because sincere believers do get deceived and get pulled away and get wrapped up in stuff for long seasons of time. Yet other people, no matter how zealous and plugged in it seemed like they may have been, the fact that they fell to this deception and got pulled away makes one wonder. This brings up the topic of eternal security.

Eternal Security

This is a great reminder. The common question asked in a Q&A is, "Do you believe in once-saved, always saved?" The answer is no—not if what people mean by that is, "Do you believe that someone can profess they believe in Jesus and then go live however they want and still be a Christian?" That is not believed.

There is no belief in a doctrine that lets us sit fat and happy while loved ones are in sin because of some singular event that happened once. But the doctrine of eternal security is for the believer. It is for no one but you. It is a doctrine that you never have to worry about your salvation. You never have to fear that you are going to be kicked out or stolen away. And that is a beautiful thing.

> *"Most assuredly, I say to you, he who hears My word and believes in Him who sent Me has everlasting life, and shall not come into judgment, but has passed from death into life." (John 5:24)*

Jesus says that the person who believes has everlasting life—is in possession of everlasting life. This person shall not ever come into judgment, but has passed from death into life.

Peter says:

> *"Having been born again, not of corruptible seed but incorruptible, through the word of God which lives and abides forever." (1 Pet. 1:23)*

You have been born again. John 3:3 says you must be born again. There are multiple born-again verses. Ephesians 1:5 is one of many verses that talk about how we have been predestined to adoption as sons by Jesus Christ Himself according to the good pleasure of His will. Romans 8 talks about adoption. Other places mention that we get adopted. We become His kids officially on paper. When we become born again, it is like the paperwork is signed and God adopts us into His family.

Although it is a promise to Israel, there is a picture in Ezekiel 36 when it talks about "I will give you a new heart and put a new spirit within you; I will take the heart of stone out of your flesh and give you a heart of flesh" (Ezek. 36:26). This is a picture of being born again.

Summarizing these verses, the Bible speaks about passing from death to life, but never life to death. The direction goes this way. There has never been a verse found that talks about passing from life into death. There is talk about rebirth, but no talk about re-death. There is talk about adoption, but never about emancipation nor excommunication where God says, "You know what? You are no longer My kids." Believers hear about our heart of stone replaced with flesh, but never reinstalling the stone.

One great way of thinking about it is this: If you realized you needed a heart transplant, your heart is dying and you do not have long to live. None of us could replace our own heart. But if you found a doctor who was willing and able to take out your heart and put in a living heart that would keep you alive, that would be a great thing. He freely offers. You receive that wonderful offer. You get to participate. You choose, because he is not going to do it if you say no. But if you sign up and you go in and you get that heart transplant and he puts that new heart in you, you are alive now.

77

But what if you decide one day, I do not like this heart anymore. I want my old dead heart back. Is there any doctor in the world who is going to give you your old dying heart back? What if you really, really, really want it back? He is like, "No, I love you too much. I am not going to give you the old heart back."

Prodigals and False Converts

It is important to also point out two other things the Bible speaks about. The Bible speaks about prodigals. The story of the prodigal son is the best example. This son who was a son told dad, "You are dead to me, give me my inheritance. I want nothing to do with you. I want to go and live life for me." The whole time he was gone with the hookers and booze and every other way he was blowing his dad's fortune, dad was looking far off, waiting for when his kid would return. Because the moment that son came to his senses that "my father might take me back," when he was yet a far off, dad was watching because he was able to throw a party together, kill the fatted calf, and get that stuff going as he ran out to meet his son.

It is that reminder that during that season, he did not look like a son. He did not act like a son. And anyone in their right mind watching him would think this guy is lost. But he was actually a son.

On the other side of that coin, the Bible speaks in multiple locations of very convincing false converts. Matthew 7:22-23 is a great example:

> *"Many will say to Me in that day, 'Lord, Lord, have we not prophesied in Your name, cast out demons in Your name, and done many wonders in Your name?' And then I will declare to them, 'I never knew you;*

depart from Me, you who practice
lawlessness!'" (Matt. 7:22-23)

Emphasis should be placed on "I never knew you."

Bringing all these things up does this: It should leave believers with a great peace and assurance about eternal security, but with a healthy sobriety concerning other people. Believers can rest assured. There are prodigals and people who backslide. The Corinthians sure did not look like Christians, but Paul called them Christians and he called them brethren, though they were living crazy lives. On the other side, there are these people over here that sure look really Christian, but Jesus said He never knew them.

It just reminds believers that they should always be discerning, always be tactful. Once again, leaning on the Holy Spirit, not banking on some past experience where, "Well, this person gave their life to Jesus at fifth-grade summer camp." You just look at where that person is at now and evaluate the situation right here and now.

If they are your son, your brother, your dad, you will probably have a little bit more hope. If you knew them well and really believe it was a sincere thing, you might have more hope. But we judge others by their fruit and treat them accordingly. If they are acting like an unbeliever, we fear for their soul like an unbeliever. But when believers look at themselves, John wrote in 1 John 5:13:

> *"These things I have written to you who*
> *believe in the name of the Son of God, that*
> *you may know that you have eternal life, and*
> *that you may continue to believe in the name*
> *of the Son of God." (1 John 5:13)*

Believers know they have eternal life—a life that is never ending with God that cannot be changed, cannot be taken, cannot be forsaken. Because in our weakness, God will not give up on us. And in our strongest rebellion, we do not believe we have enough power to outdo the power of the cross. And if somehow we could be lost once again, how would you then bring us back? Would Jesus die again for us? If our sin was able to outdo the cross the first time, these are big theological questions.

Calvinists and Arminians and people on either side of the spectrum when it comes to this theological discussion should all agree that believers can rest assured that they are going to be okay. And believers can rest assured that people who are not walking with the Lord—we should have a sober fear for them and a desire to bring them back to the truth, bring them back to walking in the light, and not just sit idly by when loved ones are living in sin.

These people though—again, they went out from us that it might be made manifest that none of them were of us. These were convincing people that they thought were believers, but once they left, it is like, well, that was the thing that revealed the truth. Verse 20 continues:

> *"But you have an anointing from the Holy*
> *One, and you know all things."*
> *(1 John 2:20)*

"You know all things" probably more likely means you know all that you need to know. In light of these false teachers with their gnostic deep knowledge, he is basically saying there is no essential secret knowledge that you are lacking. These guys are saying, "Well, we have got this extra knowledge." He is like, "No, you know everything you need to know."

Jesus said in John 14:26:

> *"But the Helper, the Holy Spirit, whom the*
> *Father will send in My name, He will teach*
> *you all things, and bring to your*
> *remembrance all things that I said to you."*
> *(John 14:26)*

He teaches the Scripture. He brings to remembrance the Scripture in times of need. This is one of the beautiful things of having the Holy Spirit.

Verse 21 says:

> *"I have not written to you because you do*
> *not know the truth, but because you know it,*
> *and that no lie is of the truth." (1 John 2:21)*

Again, these guys are trying to trick them, like, "Well, you do not know enough of the Bible. You do not know these deeper things. You need us to teach it to you. We are going to teach you these things that everyone else is getting wrong." He is like, "No, no, no, no. I am writing this because you guys do know the truth."

Verses 22 and 23 state:

> *"Who is a liar but he who denies that Jesus*
> *is the Christ? He is antichrist who denies the*
> *Father and the Son. Whoever denies the Son*
> *does not have the Father either; he who*
> *acknowledges the Son has the Father also."*
> *(1 John 2:22-23)*

Again, in context, he is addressing this specific issue with the gnostic heresies where they were playing down Jesus as something lesser than the Father and how they have a better way to the Father. In fact, if you go their way, you will get closer and a more accurate way to the Father. And he says,

81

"No, no, no, no. Without the Son, you do not have the Father at all."

Cerinthus was a contemporary of John. He was around in the 90s. Again, Cerinthianism is that teaching that Jesus was just a man. He was not Himself the Messiah. Jesus was not fully the Messiah Himself, but the spirit of Messiah, the Christ spirit, came upon Jesus at His baptism and left Him in the garden of Gethsemane or on the cross before He died. So Cerinthus taught that He is not the Christ. He just had the Christ spirit for a season. So John is saying if you deny that Jesus is the Christ, you are an antichrist. And if you deny the Son, you have no access to the Father at all. John is addressing these specific issues here.

Abiding in Truth

Verse 24 continues:

> *"Therefore let that abide in you which you heard from the beginning. If what you heard from the beginning abides in you, you also will abide in the Son and in the Father. And this is the promise that He has promised us—eternal life." (1 John 2:24-25)*

Let that abide in you which you heard from the beginning—the love of one another, the love of God. If that abides in you, you will also abide in the Son and the Father. And this is the promise that He has promised us—eternal life. That is life everlasting. That is the promise He has given us. Not a maybe life everlasting, but He is giving you life everlasting.

Verse 26 states:

> *"These things I have written to you
> concerning those who try to deceive you."
> (1 John 2:26)*

Believers need to remember that today there still are people out there really trying to deceive people. People are getting sucked out of the church. When that is said, it does not mean going from our church and joining a different church in town, but they leave the established church and end up at a fringe group.

Verse 27:

> *"But the anointing which you have received
> from Him abides in you, and you do not
> need that anyone teach you; but as the same
> anointing teaches you concerning all things,
> and is true, and is not a lie, and just as it
> has taught you, you will abide in Him."
> (1 John 2:27)*

It is always interesting reading this because many people have explained that one of the reasons they do not go to church and do not need a pastor is because the Bible says you do not need that anyone teach you. But why did John even write the letter then? There is obviously a context to this saying, because if you have no need for any teaching at all, then all these letters of the New Testament were pointless. And God was foolish to come up with a spiritual gift of teaching and the calling of the apostle, prophet, evangelist, and pastor-teacher. If there is no need for teaching, why did God create the calling and the gifting?

What it does mean is this: You are able to be a Berean, search the Scriptures for yourself, and interpret them for yourselves. You are able to read the Bible on your own and understand it on your own. You do not need—there is no necessity for some other person to tell you, "This is what the Scripture means." It does not mean there is no value in having teachers. Acts 17:11 speaks of the Bereans:

> *"These were more fair-minded than those in*
> *Thessalonica, in that they received the word*
> *with all readiness, and searched the*
> *Scriptures daily to find out whether these*
> *things were so." (Acts 17:11)*

These were the Bereans. There is a very Christian phrase: Be a Berean. Be someone who when you hear the word, you receive the word with all readiness, and then you go double-check what was said—search the Scriptures and compare Scripture to Scripture. Believers are encouraged to do this.

John wrote Scripture so that others could read it and know. That is what should be emphasized. John wrote so that we could read and know. This is a theme throughout the Scriptures—that God wrote them so that all of us could read and know. Some have promoted the idea that you cannot know the Bible without them interpreting it for you—that we need to tell you what these verses mean. That just does not work that way. The Holy Spirit will tell you. You read it.

What if people understand it differently? Well, seek the Lord some more. Seek the Holy Spirit some more. First Corinthians 4:6 says:

> *"Now these things, brethren, I have*
> *figuratively transferred to myself and*
> *Apollos for your sakes, that you may learn*
> *in us not to think beyond what is written,*
> *that none of you may be puffed up on behalf*
> *of one against the other." (1 Cor. 4:6)*

Paul is saying, "I do not want you guys to go beyond the Scripture. Stick with what is written. You do not need something beyond what is written."

Second Peter 1:20-21 says:

> *"Knowing this first, that no prophecy of Scripture is of any private interpretation, for prophecy never came by the will of man, but holy men of God spoke as they were moved by the Holy Spirit." (2 Pet. 1:20-21)*

There is no part of the Scriptures at all that has this secret interpretation that you need a special person to reveal to you.

Second Timothy 3:16-17 states:

> *"All Scripture is given by inspiration of God, and is profitable for doctrine, for reproof, for correction, for instruction in righteousness, that the man of God may be complete, thoroughly equipped for every good work." (2 Tim. 3:16-17)*

In short, you have no need for someone to teach you in that you are unable to open up your Bible and learn it for yourself. If there was no use to a teacher, then God would not have the gift and He would not have the calling. There is a lot of good use for teachers. But this is the protection that John is giving here to remind believers there is a great benefit to teachers. And we should be thankful for the teachers God has raised up. But on the other side of the coin, it is that reminder that we do not need someone to tell us what the Bible says. You can read it for yourself, and the Holy Spirit will lead and guide you just as He leads and guides everyone else.

Verses 28 and 29 close the chapter:

> *"And now, little children, abide in Him, that*
> *when He appears, we may have confidence*
> *and not be ashamed before Him at His*
> *coming. If you know that He is righteous,*
> *you know that everyone who practices*
> *righteousness is born of Him."*
> *(1 John 2:28-29)*

If we abide in Jesus, there is no reason to be ashamed at all. Believers can have a great confidence that when He shows up, they are exactly where they are supposed to be—in Him. But we all also know that when we are not abiding in Him, when we are giving into the flesh, the world, the devil, we find ourselves doing things or living in such a way that we would be ashamed if we had to stand before Him at this very moment. "What have you been doing?" "Nothing of any value, Lord." We wish we had been focusing more on Him and how to redeem the time.

If you know that He is righteous, you know that everyone who practices righteousness is born of Him. He is reminding us again: Is that person born again or not? Well, look at the people who are walking in righteousness. Deep down, the people who are born again are typically going to be seen walking in righteousness. There are prodigals, there is backsliding—that is true. But the general rule is that believers are going to see people who are going to put their money where their mouth is, and they are going to walk the walk that matches their talk.

Conclusion

John's exhortation to abide in Christ brings together all the themes of this passage. Believers are reminded that they live in the last hour, a time when Christ could return at any moment. This reality should shape how they live, how they love, and what they treasure. The doctrine of imminency is not meant to create anxiety but to foster vigilance and purpose.

The warning about antichrists—both the many who have come and the one who is yet to come—serves as a reminder that false teaching and deception are real threats. But believers are not left defenseless. They have the anointing of the Holy Spirit, the truth of God's Word, and the promise of eternal life. These are not uncertain hopes but settled realities for those who are in Christ.

The truth about eternal security should bring great comfort. Those who are truly born again can rest in the knowledge that they have passed from death to life, that they have been adopted into God's family, and that nothing can separate them from the love of God in Christ Jesus. This is not a license for careless living but a foundation for confident obedience.

At the same time, believers must maintain a sober awareness regarding others. Not everyone who claims to know Christ truly knows Him. Not everyone who appears to be a believer will endure to the end. The departure of false teachers from the church reveals their true nature— they were never truly of us. This should lead believers to examine fruit, to discern carefully, and to pray earnestly for those who seem to be wandering from the truth.

John's reminder that believers do not need anyone to teach them is not a dismissal of teaching ministry but an affirmation that the Holy Spirit enables every believer to understand Scripture. God has given teachers to the church as a gift, but He has also given His Spirit to each believer so that they can read, understand, and apply His Word for themselves. This should produce both gratitude for godly teachers and confidence in personal Bible study.

The call to abide in Christ is ultimately a call to remain in fellowship with Him, to walk in obedience to His commands, and to love Him above all else. When believers abide in Him, they need not fear His coming. They can stand before Him with confidence, knowing they are found in Him, not because of their own righteousness but because of His.

As this chapter closes, believers are left with both a warning and a promise. The warning: do not love the world or the things in the world. The promise: he who does the will of God abides forever. The world is passing away, along with all its lusts and enticements. But those who are in Christ, who walk in His truth, who love what He loves and hate what He hates—they will remain forever.

The question for each believer is simple: Are you abiding in Him? When He appears, will you have confidence, or will you be ashamed? The answer depends not on perfect performance but on whether your heart is truly His, whether His Word abides in you, and whether you are walking in the truth. John's letter is a call to examine these things honestly, to turn from anything that competes with Christ, and to live each day in light of eternity.

Abide in Him. Walk in the truth. Love what is eternal. And when He appears, you will stand before Him with confidence, knowing that you are His and He is yours, now and forever.

Children of God
1 John 3:1-3

What a privilege it is to be a child of God! Yet what are those privileges, and what does this relationship with Him entail?

To set the context for this chapter, it helps to back up slightly into the closing verses of chapter 2 to gain momentum moving into chapter 3. John writes:

> *"And now, little children, abide in Him, that*
> *when He appears we may have confidence*
> *and not be ashamed before Him at His*
> *coming. If you know that He is righteous,*
> *you know that everyone who practices*
> *righteousness is born of Him."*
> (1 John 2:28–29)

Looking at how John's letter is structured, one notices that with nearly every chapter transition, there is a verse or two that probably belonged in the next chapter. As John finishes his thoughts from chapter 2, he makes the point that we walk in the light if we are His children and that we obey His commandments if we say we love Him. In verse 29, he writes that if we know He is righteous, we know that everyone who practices righteousness is born of God. This phrase seems to have lit a light bulb in John's mind, reminding him of something important he wanted to address. And so he exclaims: "Behold what manner of love the Father has bestowed on us!"

Charles Spurgeon, in his commentary on this chapter, captures the significance of this word *behold*: "'Behold!' says he, 'read other Scriptures if you like with a glance, but stop here. I have put up a way-mark to tell you there is something eminently worthy of attention buried beneath these words.'" The idea is that *behold* is something to get our attention. Spurgeon was speaking on behalf of John, as if to say, "I'm putting this here so you can take some time to chew on this thought." Behold what manner of love the Father has bestowed on us.

The Love of God

> *"And now, little children, abide in Him, that when He appears we may have confidence and not be ashamed before Him at His coming. If you know that He is righteous, you know that everyone who practices righteousness is born of Him. Behold what manner of love the Father has bestowed on us, that we should be called children of God! Therefore the world does not know us, because it did not know Him. Beloved, now we are children of God; and it has not yet been revealed what we shall be, but we know that when He is revealed, we shall be like Him, for we shall see Him as He is. And everyone who has this hope in Him purifies himself, just as He is pure."* (1 John 3:1-3:3)

The love referenced here is *agape* (ἀγάπη) love—the biblical kind of love that Scripture speaks most about. *Agape* love is sometimes called God's love because it is the kind of love that God shows to us: His sacrificial, *agape* love.

When the text says "what manner of love," that phrase translates a single Greek word: *potapos* (ποταπός). It is a combination of the Greek words for "what" and "which," and it describes something foreign, as if to say, "Where is this coming from? We are unfamiliar with this. This is not normal and natural." The idea is that God's love is not natural to us. What makes *agape* love different from other kinds of love is that it is purely sacrificial. It is purely a gift, poured out undeservedly upon the recipient. We do not earn God's love—if we earned it, it would be a payment. And it is not merely a feeling, because feelings change. This *agape* love is a choice. It is an action, a verb— something we do and something God does. But He wants us to take a moment to chew on this: What manner of love is this?

As Christians mature, we will grow. The Bible tells us that we can grow in the grace and knowledge of the Lord Jesus. But we are also warned that we can grow cold, that we can grow dull. And quite often, that is the case—especially concerning the love of God. When we were born again, when we first became Christians, it was fresh, it was new, it was exciting. Just like falling in love—when you find someone, all of a sudden you start doing all these things you did not do before because now you are in love and you want to change. But over time, it can grow old, which is sad because that is not the way it should be.

It has been said that you can gauge the maturity of a Christian by their understanding and appreciation of the love of God. If you are growing in the right way, you will grow to love it more, to appreciate it more, to see your need of it even more. But if you are growing cold, you become more self-dependent, thinking about yourself, and God's love becomes old news. But no one wants their spouse to tell them, "Your love? It's old news. I used to care that you love me, but at this point, it's not a big deal to me anymore." God's love is special, and it is something we can spend much time focusing on. In fact, the entire book of First John centers on love—it is one of the main topics in these chapters.

The Sacrificial Nature of God's Love

Looking at what the Bible has to say about the love of God provides a good review for us. Ephesians 5:25 is a good place to start because it paints a picture:

> *"Husbands, love your wives, just as Christ also loved the church and gave Himself for her."* (Ephesians 5:25)

This is a command. And notice that *agape* love is sacrificial in nature. It is not how Jesus felt about the church; it is what He chose to do for the church. He sacrificed. He gave Himself.

With no contradiction, John 3:16 affirms the same truth:

> *"For God so loved the world that He gave His only begotten Son, that whoever believes in Him should not perish but have everlasting life."* (John 3:16)

Again, the Bible always attaches this idea of sacrifice and giving with *agape* love.

We can go all the way back to the beginning. Genesis 22:2 is the first place in the Bible where the word "love" appears:

> *"Then He said, 'Take now your son, your only son Isaac, whom you love, and go to the land of Moriah, and offer him there as a burnt offering on one of the mountains of which I shall tell you.'"* (Genesis 22:2)

If you travel to Jerusalem, you will find several prominent hilltops. There is Zion, but the main one is Moriah. If you walk up Moriah, the lower part is the old town of Salem— that is what it was called in Genesis 22. As you work your way up the hill, you pass the City of David and the Temple Mount. But the top of Mount Moriah is Calvary, Golgotha—the place where Jesus was crucified. From the very beginning, God was giving us a picture. Abraham was told to take his one and only son whom he loved and sacrifice him. God would then later send His one and only Son and sacrifice Him. The love of God is always tied with sacrifice—it is tied with what God has done for us.

The Greatness of God's Love

The Bible speaks of the greatness of God's love—it is awesome. And this theme runs through both Old and New Testaments. It is a sad thing when people claim that the God of the Old Testament is somehow different from the God of the New Testament. Such people have never truly read both testaments, because if you read them both, it is the same God from beginning to end.

> *"...His great love with which He loved us."*
> (Ephesians 2:4)

Jeremiah, which is admittedly a gloomy book amidst all the judgment and all the things happening, contains this beautiful declaration:

> *"The LORD has appeared of old to me,*
> *saying: 'Yes, I have loved you with an*
> *everlasting love; therefore with*
> *lovingkindness I have drawn you.'"*
> (Jeremiah 31:3)

God is speaking through Jeremiah to the people of Israel. He is trying to win them over. Ephesians 3:19 adds:

> *"...to know the love of Christ which passes*
> *knowledge; that you may be filled with all*
> *the fullness of God."* (Ephesians 3:19)

93

This love is drawing us—this great love. And so in chapter 4 of First John, we read, "We love Him because He first loved us" (1 John 4:19). That is the idea again in Jeremiah: "With lovingkindness I am drawing you." With His love, He draws us. Romans 2:4, paraphrasing slightly, has Paul basically saying, "Do you not realize, do you not know, that it is the goodness of God that leads you to repentance?"

It is God's love which He gives us and pours out on us that often brings us back. That is often what gets us home. So many people have shared how they were struggling with sin and could not get free. They tried harder and harder and harder. But what really set them free was the goodness of God, the grace of God. When they realized that they were forgiven the moment they sinned, all of a sudden they had strength they did not have before. It is not the fear of judgment. It is realizing that God loves them even when they mess up.

> *"But God demonstrates His own love*
> *toward us, in that while we were still*
> *sinners, Christ died for us."* (Romans 5:8)

If God loved us then, why would He ever stop loving us now? That is often a deception the devil would love to use: "I have just failed God and messed up so much. He probably does not love me anymore." But no—He declared and sent His Son to die for us when we were rejecting Him, when we were in rebellion, living life for ourselves and not caring about God. That is the person He showed His love to. So now that we are living for Him and we made a mistake or have been struggling through something, do we really think He is going to stop? It is not consistent. God has a love that does not change, that is not conditional. It is the most long-suffering love you could ever imagine.

A Picture of Unfailing Love

God wanted to paint a picture for the Old Testament people of Israel. He had a prophet named Hosea, and He told Hosea to marry a prostitute. So Hosea married this woman, and they had some children. But then she left him to go back into prostitution.

> *"Then the LORD said to me, 'Go again, love a woman who is loved by a lover and is committing adultery, just like the love of the LORD for the children of Israel, who look to other gods and love the raisin cakes of the pagans.'"* (Hosea 3:1)

Israel was getting into all this pagan practice; they were in spiritual adultery. But God's love is greater than that. He says, "I want you, Hosea, to have this unfaithful wife. She is going to leave you and go back into her old ways of prostitution, but I want you to take her back—because that can show people how much I love them." Even amidst perhaps the greatest betrayal, God says, "I will still take you back because I love you."

And God is love. First John 4:8 declares, "He who does not love does not know God, for God is love." We have probably heard it said—sometimes we forget where the Bible says it—but this is where it says it. God is love.

Just as God is holy—we use God to define what holiness is, because in God there is nothing bad, nothing wrong, there is no sin; He is perfectly holy—and just as God is just—everything about Him is perfect justice; whatever decision He makes, that is the right decision, and it is how we know what right decisions are—so too God is love. Because God is love, everything He ever does will be loving. Everything He does is our model of what love looks like. If we want to know how to love people better, we look to Him, because God is love.

God Is Love

What is wonderful is that, knowing God is love, we can take Bible verses that tell us about what love is, and they are essentially telling us what God is. When we look at 1 Corinthians 13, the love chapter, we can substitute God's name in place of love:

God suffers long and is kind. God does not envy. God does not parade Himself, is not puffed up. God does not behave rudely, does not seek His own, is not provoked, thinks no evil. God does not rejoice in iniquity, but rejoices in the truth. God bears all things, believes all things, hopes all things, endures all things. God's love never fails.

It does not work when you put your name in there—notice that. Whenever you put your own name in there, everything falls apart. But when you put God in there, it makes sense. He does suffer long. He is kind.

Some unbelievers say, "I do not believe in a God who wants to force people to worship Him," as if God were on some ego trip. But God is not on an ego trip. In fact, He is simply trying to find people who will receive His love—not demanding all these things out of them.

Notice that in the middle of that passage, we read that God is not provoked. Because He demonstrated His own love for us in that while we were still sinners, Christ died for us. Because God loved us when we were sinners, because God loved us while we were still actively sinning and rebelling, we can know that He will never stop loving us.

We have high seasons and low seasons. We feel really good, then we feel really bad. But the reality is that God is unchanging. He never changes. And because He never changes and He already said He loves you, consider this: chances are that today is not the day that you feel the most loved by God you have ever felt in your whole life. If it is, congratulations—God bless you. But we have ups and downs. How close we feel, how loved we feel, how much we are embracing God's love—it has its highs and its lows. But we need to remember that the day we felt the most loved, when everything was perfect in our relationship with God, the reality is twofold: first, He actually loved us even more than we comprehended on that day; and second, even when we feel at our worst, He has not changed from that day. When we really felt loved and accepted, He has never loved us less. He has never accepted us less, because God does not change.

When it says that God is not provoked, we need to remember that when we accepted His gift of love, He already knew everything we would do. He already knew, "She is going to end up doing this; she is going to go off and do that; he is going to fail here—in fact, he is going to fail here time and time again." And God said, "Yes, I already know all that. I want to love them and I want to save them." You cannot provoke a God who knows the future. You cannot provoke a God who saw everything that was already coming. His love outdoes all these things.

God Knows, and His Love Never Fails

At the end of that little love section in 1 Corinthians, we read that love bears all things, believes all things, hopes all things, endures all things. In the actual verse, where it says love believes and hopes for the best in all situations, we need to remember something about God: He does believe

97

and hope the best because He knows the truth. He is all-knowing. He knows how the story is going to end. He knows your heart when you mess up. He knows how much it frustrates you.

It is interesting—you might have to convince your friends, you might have to convince your family, but you do not have to convince God of the truth. When you say, "Lord, if I could just flip a switch and never do that again, I would be so on board. God, if I could just stop sinning—" God knows. He says, "Yes, I know you would, but that is not how it works. You are going to learn some things. And every time you stumble, I am going to teach you a new lesson." He knows all these things.

And the very end of that passage declares that God's love never fails. He is perfect in power, perfect in authority. His love has nothing stopping it from doing what He set out to do.

But the reality is that not everyone will receive God's love. Some people question, "Does that mean God's love does not work, or did it fail?" No, because God pours out His love on everyone, knowing that not everyone will love Him in return as He desires.

What if God could just take away sin? Well, He would have to take away us—that is the only way to really get rid of all the sin in the world, to get rid of all the people sinning. That does not work. What if God could just make it so we could not sin? That does not really work either. Why did God make mankind? I do not think He made us to worship Him—I do not see that in the Bible. We are the object of His love. He made us to love us, but also that we would love Him in return.

If God made mankind with no option other than to love
Him, He basically would have made a bunch of robot
people—like a computer program that when you say,
"Love me," it says, "I love you. I love you. I love you."
Maybe your two-year-old likes their little stuffed animal
that says, "I love you," when you squeeze it. But I do not
know if any of us get a whole lot of satisfaction out of that.
When you are having a bad day, you do not go squeeze the
teddy bear and say, "Okay, everything is better now. The
teddy bear loves me."

But that same two-year-old, when they have just barely
learned to talk, and out of the blue they say, "I love you,
Dad"—that hits. Because you know they did not have to
say that. Nothing was making them say that. They were
choosing to love you.

Or consider a baby who cannot even talk yet. You are
sitting there holding and patting the baby, and all of a
sudden they start patting your back. There is something
special about that. I confess, I have had many babies, and I
find little babies to be somewhat boring—that is just me. I
am waiting to play ball or run around or do something with
them. They just lie there. But then they start interacting. I
want to interact with my kids. I am excited to do something
with them. With my youngest daughter, she is so stoic most
of the time—she just stares. I keep saying, "Smile! Do
something! I want interaction!" Because it is a real
relationship then.

God made us with the ability to love Him in return or reject
Him, because if we did not have the choice to reject His
love, it would not really be love. This is the love of God.
He made us to love us so that we could love Him in return
and have a relationship with Him.

That We Should Be Called Children of God

The text says, "Behold what manner of love the Father has bestowed on us." Notice the word "Father" here—this was revolutionary in the New Testament. In the Old Testament, there was occasionally a husband-wife analogy used for God and His people, though not very common. But what you really do not find is the idea that God was our Father. The only place you will find it is in Isaiah, in one of the Christmas verses: "And His name shall be called Wonderful, Counselor, Mighty God, Everlasting Father" (Isaiah 9:6).

We are told in that one prophetic verse about the Messiah—which is interesting because there is Jesus, and there is the Father, and it is all getting tied together in that one verse. But that is the only place in the Old Testament where this is even obscurely referenced. Then Jesus, when He began teaching in the Sermon on the Mount, began saying it again and again: "You need to be salt and light so that when people see your good works, it will glorify your Father in heaven." "You want to pray? Well, this is how you pray: Our Father who art in heaven, hallowed be Your name." "Be perfect as your Father in heaven is perfect." He kept saying "your Father, your Father." This idea of being God's children was a new thing.

People were surprised because in the past, God had actually been somewhat distant—this holy God who is so far away because He is so holy and we are not. There was a great distance. But what we find now is different. No, we do not need to have that distance. We can boldly go before the throne of grace because we are God's children. We have access because we are His children.

And so the text declares that we should be called the children of God. This tells us even more about God's love, because it is not just any love. It is agape love, but even more specifically, it is the love of a father or a mother for their child.

Parental Love Is the Strongest of All Loves

First, parental love is probably the strongest of all loves. You might have to think and evaluate a little bit, but while we love our spouses, that is something that grew with time, something we make as a choice. But with our children, it was always there. It was instilled inside of us. You see people get divorced—far too common these days. But you do not see a whole lot of disowned children. In fact, you see far more children trying to leave and parents wishing they would not. The parental love is a strong love.

> *"...then they will look on Me whom they pierced. Yes, they will mourn for Him as one mourns for his only son, and grieve for Him as one grieves for a firstborn."* (Zechariah 12:10)

This picture was being used because, well, what greater pain could someone have other than the loss of a child? We all know that if we stay married, either we are going to go or our spouse is going to go first. We kind of know inevitably that one spouse is going to lose the other. But God did not wire us to lose children. We live in a fallen world where it happens, and one day it will never happen again. But the pain experienced is only contrasted by the strength of the love—it would not hurt so bad if the love were not so strong. That is the kind of love God has for you. It is so very strong.

God Will Never Forsake His Children

Second, we know that God will never forsake His children. Parents just do not forsake their children. Yes, in this fallen world there are some wicked sinners who go against the norm, but the average human being—it does not really matter what our children do—we always take them back. We always take them home.

In the story of the prodigal son in Luke 15, there is that young man who tells his father—and the way you can summarize it is he tells his father, "Dad, I want nothing to do with you. I want you as dead to me. Therefore, I can get my inheritance and just get out of this place." And you will note the father does it—he is not forcing him to stay. He is not forcing his children. "Okay, I am dead to you. Here is the money. You can go."

And the young man goes off—whether it is drinking, immorality, gambling, whatever—he goes off and spends it all. Prodigal living is where we get the term. He lived this life of just blowing it on whatever he wanted, filling every one of his desires. But when he came to his senses and thought, "Maybe Dad will take me back if I come home," the Bible tells us that, seeing him from far off, the father went out, had the fatted calf killed, and started throwing a party.

That detail—seeing him from far off—reminds us that the dad was watching. The father was watching and waiting for his son's return. In that culture, you could not have done anything more insulting to your parents than what that young man did. But God is always ready to take His children home. He is always excited to take His children home. It is a great reminder that with this parental love of God, we are His children. He is not kicking us out. And no matter how horribly we betray Him, if we are faithless, He remains faithful. These are beautiful promises.

God Will Perfectly Parent Us

Third, because we are God's children, we can expect that God will perfectly parent us. Every command that the Bible has on parenting, we can expect that God will do those things. He is not going to shortchange us. He will not tell earthly fathers, "Be this way as a father," and then Himself be different. He is going to do the exact same things.

> *"And you, fathers, do not provoke your children to wrath, but bring them up in the training and admonition of the Lord."*
> (Ephesians 6:4)

Colossians adds, "lest they become discouraged." This is a good reminder that God is never trying to provoke us. God is never trying to discourage us, because He is perfect and holy. He will not command earthly fathers to do one thing and then go do another. God is not a hypocrite.

So we can be reminded that whatever He is putting us through, it is never to provoke us—it is to challenge us and to grow us. Whatever we are going through, He is not intending for us to become discouraged. Though there is an enemy who would love to twist any situation to discourage us, God is challenging us and putting us through things as a loving father would. Loving fathers do not just make everything easy for their children. They push their children. They challenge their children. They train their children. They make their children do hard things so their children can learn and grow. That is what our Father in heaven is doing with us.

*"You shall teach them diligently to your
children, and shall talk of them when you sit
in your house, when you walk by the way,
when you lie down, and when you rise up."*
(Deuteronomy 6:7)

This comes after God gave the Ten Commandments in
Deuteronomy 5 and the Shema in Deuteronomy 6: "Hear,
O Israel: the LORD your God, the LORD is one. You shall
love the LORD your God with all your heart, with all your
soul, and with all your strength." He then tells parents to
teach all this—His laws and His commands to love Him,
the whole of it—diligently to their children. They should be
going over this material again and again and again. The
interesting thing is that in the Hebrew, "teach them
diligently" is one Hebrew word: *shannan*. It is only found
here translated as "to teach." Everywhere else in the Old
Testament, it is the word for sharpening a sword with a
whetstone—you have a stone and you are sharpening the
sword. Some of us are very dull swords, and it takes many
repetitive strokes again and again and again to sharpen us
up. But that is what God will do with us. He will teach us
these lessons repeatedly. He is diligent and He is not
quitting. He is just going to keep teaching and keep going.
It might be a long and slow process, but He is faithfully
working in our lives because He is a faithful Father.

The Discipline of a Loving Father

Hebrews chapter 12 speaks powerfully about God being
our Father and how He deals with us because He is our
Father:

*"My son, do not despise the chastening of
the LORD, nor be discouraged when you are
rebuked by Him; for whom the LORD loves
He chastens, and scourges every son whom*

*He receives. If you endure chastening, God
deals with you as with sons. For what son is
there whom a father does not chasten? But if
you are without chastening, of which all
have become partakers, then you are
illegitimate and not sons. Furthermore, we
have had human fathers who corrected us,
and we paid them respect. Shall we not
much more readily be in subjection to the
Father of spirits and live? For they indeed
for a few days chastened us as seemed best
to them, but He for our profit, that we may
be partakers of His holiness. Now no
chastening seems to be joyful for the
present, but painful; nevertheless, afterward
it yields the peaceable fruit of righteousness
to those who have been trained by it."*
(Hebrews 12:5–11)

The writer of Hebrews points out that every father chastens
his children—because that is what good fathers do. That is
what a loving father does. In fact, Proverbs says, "He who
spares the rod hates his son, but he who loves him
disciplines him promptly" (Proverbs 13:24). What children
are there whose fathers do not discipline them?

Furthermore, if we could just keep on sinning in life
without there being consequences—well, if God is our
Father, there are going to be consequences. The scary
thought is this: if someone could just keep on sinning and
there are never consequences, well, maybe they are an
illegitimate child. Maybe He is not really their Father.

The passage also reminds us that we had human fathers
who corrected us, and we paid them respect. Shall we not
much more readily be in subjection to the Father of spirits
and live? Our earthly fathers chastened us for a few days as

seemed best to them, but our heavenly Father chastens us for our profit, that we may be partakers of His holiness. God is doing it for a reason. No chastening seems joyful at the present—it is painful. But afterward it yields the peaceable fruit of righteousness to those who have been trained by it.

God loves us as a Father. It is a powerful love. It is a faithful love. And it is a love that includes tough love and lessons. As we study the Bible and learn how to be good parents, we actually learn a great deal about how God parents us. And we can flip that around: learning about how God parents us teaches us how we should be parenting our own children.

So, behold what manner of love the Father has bestowed on us, that we should be called children of God! This is a special kind of love.

The World Does Not Know Us

The text continues: "Therefore the world does not know us, because it did not know Him." John continually presents these pictures of what it is like in the world versus what we should be like. Because the world rejected God, the world is going to reject us too. We are going to stand out. We are going to be different. They are not going to understand us—that is really what this is saying. This is not so much about rejection as it is about the world simply not understanding us.

This can have two sides to it. On one hand, we do not do all the bad things. We do not do this, we do not do that. And the world does not get it. "Why would you not just do it this way?" And the answer is simple: "Because it is wrong. That is why." That side often gets the focus and gets plenty of attention.

But on the other side of that coin—and this is well worth remembering—are the positives. "Why are you always so happy? How is it that you can hear such news and yet still hold it all together? Why are you so kind all the time, even when other people treat you poorly?" They do not get that, because the world does not work that way. Worldly people do not do that. But we are different. And it should make their brains hurt a little. They do not get God's children because they never got Him in the first place.

Now We Are Children of God

Verse 2 begins, "Beloved, now we are children of God." The word "now" is important to note. Now we are children of God—because we were not always. And that is important to note. Everyone is not a child of God. The idea that "we are all God's children" is not true. Everyone has the option to become one of God's children, but not everyone is.

> *"But when the fullness of the time had come, God sent forth His Son, born of a woman, born under the law, to redeem those who were under the law, that we might receive the adoption as sons."* (Galatians 4:4–5)

We are adopted children. We did not start off as His, but He made the way and He paid the price. The adoption paperwork was all done. But we had to receive it and become God's children.

> *"...having predestined us to adoption as sons by Jesus Christ to Himself, according to the good pleasure of His will."*
> (Ephesians 1:5)

God always knew how it was going to turn out. It is by Jesus Christ, to Himself, according to the good pleasure of His will.

Biological children are yours whether you like it or not. Many people have had children by accident—it was not intentional, they were not trying to get pregnant, and all of a sudden it happened. And then they are your children. But no one adopts a child on accident. No one goes off for a crazy weekend in Las Vegas and comes back with three adopted children. It just does not work that way. Adoption is a choice. It is a process. It is a commitment. And it is very much an act of love—"I am choosing to make you my child."

The reality is that God chose us to be His children. He wanted us to be His children.

> *"...but you received the Spirit of adoption by whom we cry out, 'Abba, Father.'"* (Romans 8:15)

We get to be adopted. We were not His children, but now we are the children of God. When we became Christians, we became one of God's children.

We Shall Be Like Him

The text continues: "And it has not yet been revealed what we shall be, but we know that when He is revealed, we shall be like Him, for we shall see Him as He is." We do not fully know what this end result is going to look like, but we do know that when He is revealed, we shall be like Him.

> *"Therefore be imitators of God as dear children."* (Ephesians 5:1)

The first thing we see is that, as we become Christians, we try to become more like Him in little things. We are growing in grace. We are growing to become more like God. Sanctification is taking place. But one day we are going to be transformed.

> *"For our citizenship is in heaven, from which we also eagerly wait for the Savior, the Lord Jesus Christ, who will transform our lowly body that it may be conformed to His glorious body, according to the working by which He is able even to subdue all things to Himself."* (Philippians 3:20–21)

The idea is that right now, we are in a certain package. It has its issues. It is falling apart. It likes to sin. But one day we will be transformed to be like Jesus. When He resurrected, He had a glorified body. He could teleport into a room. He still bore the marks of His suffering, so there were similarities, but people did not even recognize Him half the time. We do not know exactly what it is going to be like for us, but we know we will be transformed to be like Him. And if it sounds crazy, just remember that last part of the verse: He is "able even to subdue all things to Himself." Yes, He can even handle you.

> *"But we all, with unveiled face, beholding as in a mirror the glory of the Lord, are being transformed into the same image from glory to glory, just as by the Spirit of the Lord."* (2 Corinthians 3:18)

When we read the word "mirror," we think of a mirror as we know it today. But we need to remember that in that time period, they did not have mirrors anything like we have today. In Corinth, where this was written, they were famous for Corinthian bronze. They would take the metal, flatten it as well as they could, and then polish it as smoothly as possible. You would end up with a mirror where you could see your reflection, but it was not great. It was enough to see that everything was there—your hair, your face—but the image was dim. In fact, in 1 Corinthians 13:12, Paul says we see "in a mirror, dimly." The point is the same: we can get a dim idea; we vaguely understand what it is going to be like that day. But we are going to be transformed into the same image, from glory to glory, just as by the Spirit of the Lord.

All these verses say the same thing: we do not quite see what it is going to be like right now, but we know that one day we are going to be like Him. That is literal—we will literally be transformed and literally have a body similar to His, though we do not fully understand it yet.

Growing in Maturity

There is also another transformation that is currently taking place. Children grow up to be like their parents. They look like their parents. They might share their parents' laugh. They have all these traits, but we never quite know which traits they are going to get. They might end up being more like this parent or more like that parent. With babies, all my children were born and it was always the question: Are they going to have blue eyes? Are they going to have a different color? Some of my children have these green eyes that seem to change colors. Others have striking blue eyes. We do not know at first because their eyes are so dark when they are born. We wait to see what color eyes, what traits. They are all different, but we know they are going to turn out something like their mom or their dad and have a mix of traits.

As we grow up spiritually, we are going to become like God. And if we want to become like God, we can learn from what Scripture teaches about parenting. The more I learn about parenting, the more it helps me in my Christian walk.

> *"Jesus answered and said to him, 'Most assuredly, I say to you, unless one is born again, he cannot see the kingdom of God.'"* (John 3:3)

Jesus told Nicodemus that unless one is born again, he cannot see the kingdom of God. When you become a Christian, you start from ground zero—a spiritual baby—and you begin to grow. We know that babies need certain things, and the same is true for spiritual growth.

Babies Need Food

If you are a child of God and you want to grow, step one is to get well-fed.

> *"As newborn babes, desire the pure milk of the word, that you may grow thereby."* (1 Peter 2:2)

> *"It is written, 'Man shall not live by bread alone, but by every word that proceeds from the mouth of God.'"* (Matthew 4:4)

If you want to grow as God's child, get into the Word. You need that for growth.

Babies Need Their Diapers Changed

It is a reality that children continually need diaper changes, over and over and over again. And as we covered earlier in this letter, 1 John 1:9 reminds us that we do sin and we do need regular cleansing and coming before God:

> *"If we confess our sins, He is faithful and just to forgive us our sins and to cleanse us from all unrighteousness."* (1 John 1:9)

No matter how fresh the sin, no matter how rebellious, He is the faithful one. He is the just one who will forgive us our sins and cleanse us of all unrighteousness. It is good for us to keep coming back to Him again and again, having those fresh diaper changes. We need it.

Babies Need Rest

As we are growing in our maturity, we need rest.

> *"Take My yoke upon you and learn from Me, for I am gentle and lowly in heart, and you will find rest for your souls."* (Matthew 11:29)

There is real rest in Christ.

Babies Need Love

Scientifically and logically, studies have shown that you can have two babies, and both can be fed, both can be given diaper changes, both can be clothed and kept warm—all the essential things for life. But babies who are held, rocked, and receive more human touch experience a change in their brain development. They have stimulation in their brains that children who are left sitting around all the time do not develop. Love is an important part of our growth and development.

This love of God—we know about it, but we really need to be staying in it and receiving it.

> *"Keep yourselves in the love of God, looking for the mercy of our Lord Jesus Christ unto eternal life."* (Jude 21)

This is something we actively do. We actively stay in God's love, reminding ourselves of God's love, remembering how much we need God's love. It will help us grow. It will help us mature as we become bigger children of God.

Everyone Who Has This Hope Purifies Himself

Verse 3 says, "And everyone who has this hope in Him purifies himself, just as He is pure." Everything we have talked about—being God's child, knowing God's unfailing love, understanding that no matter how much we mess up or do wrong, God's love never changes—the people who get that, the text says, purify themselves just as He is pure.

This word "purify" is not a super common word in our Bibles. It is *hagnizō* (ἁγνίζω), from the same root as "holy" and "sanctify," but it is different. This word typically speaks of ceremonial cleansing. While *hagiazō* (to sanctify) is something the Bible continually talks about as the work of God in us—something He is doing—here with *hagnizō* it is just the practical. In fact, the first four times this word is mentioned in the New Testament, in the Gospels and in Acts, it speaks of men going to the mikvah to do the ritual washing. It is something that we do.

We should expect that someone who has understood the love of God and received the love of God would have a desire to clean things up. We talked about babies getting their diapers changed. Here is the reality: when a baby has a dirty diaper, you change it and that is life. When you find out that the toddler has made a mess, you get a little

113

frustrated because they are potty trained—but they had an accident, so you cut them some slack.

But when your sixteen-year-old has an accident, you are worried. Something is wrong there—especially if it happens often. No one is going to avoid seeing the doctor if their teenager is having such problems all the time. Why do I bring this up? Because this is making the point that as Christians mature, we expect this cleansing process to take place. They are growing and maturing and working these things out of themselves. It is a scary and bad sign if we see sin and filth and dirtiness showing up again and again without remorse or change.

A Gift That Must Be Received

As we sang at the beginning of our worship and as we looked at the beginning of this study, "For God so loved the world that He gave His only begotten Son" (John 3:16). He loved us, and so He gave His Son for us. God's love is a gift. But a gift must be received—and this is twofold.

First, you have to receive God's love that first time to be born again, forgiven of sins, to be adopted into His kingdom. But second, we need to remember that God did not just want to love us once. God is still loving you. He is still desiring to show His love to you. You can become a Christian and, for whatever strange reason, reject His ongoing love. Maybe you become self-sufficient. Maybe you start condemning yourself when God has not condemned you. Whatever the reason, we need to be receiving His love regularly.

As Paul wrote to the Thessalonians:

> *"Now may the Lord direct your hearts into*
> *the love of God and into the patience of*
> *Christ."* (2 Thessalonians 3:5)

That is what we want—that God would steer our ship back into His love, that we might keep ourselves in the love of God.

The Epistles of John

The Practice of Righteousness
1 John 3:4-12

Much of this chapter contains statements that are very straightforward. Many of the truths here make good sense on their own, yet John is not simply stating the obvious for its own sake. There are a few sections that require a little digging to get the best understanding, but much of what follows is direct and practical.

Sin as Lawlessness

"Whoever commits sin also commits lawlessness, and sin is lawlessness." (1 John 3:4)

On the other side of this equation, obedience to the law means not sinning. What John seems to emphasize here is a shift away from thinking about a law of rules. The Jews had so much on their minds about keeping the law—following its requirements, checking off their obligations. But it became so much about rule-keeping, crossing every t and dotting every i, that they lost sight of the deeper question: Is it sinful?

There is a very different attitude between meticulously following rules and simply asking, "Is this sin or not?" Rather than trying to define every technicality, John cuts through all of it: sin is lawlessness, lawlessness is sin. It is straightforward.

Jesus Manifested to Take Away Sin

"And you know that He was manifested to take away our sins, and in Him there is no sin." (1 John 3:5)

The word "manifest" appears several times in this chapter. To manifest something is to bring it to the surface so it can be made known. A person might have an illness, but none of the symptoms have made themselves manifest yet. When the symptoms come out, the illness becomes visible. Jesus was manifested to us because He always was—He was born of the virgin, yes, but the idea is that something already existing came into our existence so we could see Him.

He was manifested to take away our sins. The Greek word for "take away" is *airō* (αἴρω), meaning to carry away. What stands out is that in the New Testament, every time this word is spoken of a person, it is always talking about taking them to judgment—throwing someone into prison, carrying them away to face consequences. One can pick up a candlestick and set it over there without moral implications, but if the word is ever spoken of a person, it speaks of being carried away to judgment.

This brings to mind Romans 8:3:

"For what the law could not do in that it was weak through the flesh, God did by sending His own Son in the likeness of sinful flesh, on account of sin: He condemned sin in the flesh." (Romans 8:3)

Jesus took sin and carried it off to judgment. The result is that sin no longer has the power over us that it once did. Legally, it has no power because we are no longer bound by it. And practically, we are being set free from its power on a day-to-day basis.

Abiding and Not Continuing in Sin

"Whoever abides in Him does not sin. Whoever sins has neither seen Him nor known Him." (1 John 3:6)

This is the New King James translation, which is a fine translation. The King James Bible and its update sought to preserve the flow of the older English while making some elements easier to understand. But here is the challenge: in updating the language, some things were lost.

The King James Version reads: "Whosoever abideth in him sinneth not: whosoever sinneth hath not seen him, neither known him."

In Greek, there are verb tenses that we often lose in English. Unlike almost any other language—Spanish, Russian, Greek, Hebrew—English verb endings rarely change to indicate ongoing action. In those languages, the endings of words shift significantly depending on tense and aspect. The -eth ending in the King James is a present tense verb indicating ongoing action. This nuance gets lost in the New King James because translators were trying to modernize the language while keeping the flow similar.

If we are continually abiding in Him, then we are not going to be continually sinning. The ESV captures this well: "No one who abides in him keeps on sinning; no one who keeps on sinning has either seen him or known him." The translators had to add the words "keeps on," but that is exactly what the Greek verb tense means.

This concept continues through the next handful of verses. People have misunderstood 1 John 3:6 to think it says Christians do not sin. But that interpretation makes the first two chapters of 1 John nonsensical. John already wrote, "If anyone sins, he has an advocate with the Father," and "If

119

we confess our sins, He is faithful and just." Those earlier verses were written to help Christians deal with the sins John fully expected to happen.

The point is this: people who abide in Christ are not going to keep living in sin. When someone just keeps living in their sin with no sign of change or even desire for change, that is a serious warning sign. It should be sobering for those who love such people—watching someone live in sin as though there is no problem is itself a big problem.

Practicing Righteousness

"Little children, let no one deceive you. He who practices righteousness is righteous, just as He is righteous." (1 John 3:7)

Here the translators use a helpful word: "practices." One either practices sin or practices righteousness. Practice is something done repeatedly to improve—we practice at things we want to get better at, things we desire to grow in.

It makes sense that those who have been declared righteous by the blood of Jesus are the very same people we will observe practically living out righteousness. They are trying to be righteous, working at it, working toward it. Those who are practicing righteousness are working to improve—and that is a telltale sign of someone who has been declared righteous before God because of their faith in Jesus. But those who are not practicing righteousness? That is a bad sign.

Of the Devil

"He who sins is of the devil, for the devil has sinned from the beginning. For this purpose the Son of God was

manifested, that He might destroy the works of the devil."
(1 John 3:8)

Again, almost all of these verbs are present tense, indicating ongoing action. He who continues in sin is of the devil. That is why Jesus came—to put an end to the works of the devil.

The phrase "of the devil" uses the Greek word *ek* (ἐκ), meaning "out of" or "from." Jesus uses this same language in John 8:44 when He tells the religious leaders:

"You are of your father the devil, and the desires of your father you want to do. He was a murderer from the beginning, and does not stand in the truth, because there is no truth in him. When he speaks a lie, he speaks from his own resources, for he is a liar and the father of it." (John 8:44)

The people of this world have their father, in a sense. We are born into this world under the power of Satan. We are sons and daughters of the devil until we become adopted as children of God. Everyone has a father, and it is one or the other—nothing in between. This is a good reminder: there are no "good people" who are not Christians. They might be good by some earthly measure and standard, but at the end of the day, a person is either of their father the devil or of God the Father.

Born of God

"Whoever has been born of God does not sin, for His seed remains in him; and he cannot sin, because he has been born of God." (1 John 3:9)

The Greek word for "seed" here is *sperma* (σπέρμα). The English derivative is obvious. This is a very literal picture

John is using, because from the sperm comes the DNA of the father. When a child is born, the father's seed produces DNA in that child, and from that DNA come the qualities and traits of the father.

There are beautiful pictures throughout Scripture of what it means to be born of God. God designed human reproduction in a specific way—everything was intentional. And here John uses that imagery: His seed remains in us. The DNA came from the Father, was placed in us, and forms what we are going to become.

When it says "he cannot sin because he has been born of God," this is again the continuing verb—he cannot remain in sin. It does not mean we cannot sin; we know we do. But we also know we cannot stay that way, because one of two things will happen: conviction or chastisement.

When believers get caught up in sin, they become miserable. They feel far from God. All these things happen, and so they get themselves right. Or if that does not happen on its own, their sin finds them out—God sends chastisement into their lives.

Hebrews 12:7–8 addresses this directly:

"If you endure chastening, God deals with you as with sons; for what son is there whom a father does not chasten? But if you are without chastening, of which all have become partakers, then you are illegitimate and not sons." (Hebrews 12:7–8)

God chastens His children. That is fancy Bible language for giving spankings. "Whom He loves, He chastens." "He who spares the rod hates his son." Proverbs speaks repeatedly of a father chastening his son because he loves him. Believers cannot remain in sin because the chastening of the Lord will come, and it will become progressively more intense.

Discipline with children should be progressive—it does not have to start big, but if a small correction does not work, something a little more is tried. If that does not work, something more still. The goal is to bring a person to the breaking point where they begin to make right decisions. God does the same with His children. We cannot continue in sin because God will deal with us—unless we are illegitimate.

Now, that is not meant to frighten anyone. John will soon offer encouraging words about assurance. These truths are not supposed to scare the believer, but they are supposed to wake up the unbeliever. It can be difficult to balance these realities: some people need a wake-up call while others feel broken and need healing and love. The Holy Spirit must do His work, and God's Word must be allowed to accomplish its purpose. The bottom line is that God's children cannot keep living in sin forever—God will send a wake-up call and get a hold of them.

Children Made Manifest

"In this the children of God and the children of the devil are manifest: Whoever does not practice righteousness is not of God, nor is he who does not love his brother." (1 John 3:10)

Here we see the word "manifest" again, but now applied to believers and unbelievers rather than to Christ. Looking back to chapter 2, verse 19, John wrote about false teachers: "They went out from us, but they were not of us; for if they had been of us, they would have continued with us; but they went out that they might be made manifest."

First John is a spiraling book—John hits the same topics repeatedly with slightly different wording, driving home a few essential points. The children of God and the children of the devil are made manifest by their works. "By their fruit you shall know them." James speaks of someone with a proclaimed faith that has no visible works as having a dead faith—a faith that does not save.

It is not the works that save; it is the works that show someone is saved. This is simple but essential. When examining someone's life, if their profession of faith does not match their practice, it raises serious questions. And this should be expressed with love and compassion and godly fear—with meekness and fear, as Peter says, being ready to give a defense and an answer for the hope we have. A sincere concern about someone's salvation based on what their life reveals is appropriate.

Notice how John pairs two things in this verse: practicing righteousness by ourselves, and loving our brothers in relation to others. These are the two dimensions—sins in isolation and sins involving other people. The children of God are both working at being righteous and loving their brothers and sisters.

Love One Another

"For this is the message that you heard from the beginning, that we should love one another." (1 John 3:11)

This connects back to chapter 2, verse 24: "Therefore let that abide in you which you heard from the beginning." And chapter 2, verses 7–8: "I write no new commandment to you, but an old commandment which you have had from the beginning. The old commandment is the word which you heard from the beginning."

John keeps emphasizing this point like a broken record, and he does so intentionally. He sounds repetitive because he wants his readers to actually start doing what he has told them to do. There is an old story of a pastor who kept saying week after week, "Little children, love one another." When people finally asked why, he replied, "I'm just waiting for you to start doing it. I'll keep saying the same thing over and over until we start seeing this happen."

This is the message from the beginning. It is not going to change.

The Example of Cain

"Not as Cain who was of the wicked one and murdered his brother. And why did he murder him? Because his works were evil and his brother's righteous." (1 John 3:12)

John points to Cain as a counter-example to loving one's brother. Turning to Genesis 4, most know the story, but examining the details reveals truths that do not always stand out.

"Now Adam knew Eve his wife, and she conceived and bore Cain, and said, 'I have acquired a man from the LORD.' Then she bore again, this time his brother Abel. Now Abel was a keeper of sheep, but Cain was a tiller of the ground. And in the process of time it came to pass that Cain brought an offering of the fruit of the ground to the LORD. Abel also brought of the firstborn of his flock and of their fat. And the LORD respected Abel and his offering, but He did not respect Cain and his offering. And Cain was very angry, and his countenance fell." (Genesis 4:1–5)

Notice that it says God respected Abel and his offering, but did not respect Cain nor his offering. It was not just about the offerings—it was about the men themselves. As

125

children hearing Bible stories, we might wonder what was wrong with what Cain brought. But the text does not just say God disliked what Cain brought; it was Cain himself whom God did not accept.

"So the LORD said to Cain, 'Why are you angry? And why has your countenance fallen? If you do well, will you not be accepted? And if you do not do well, sin lies at the door. And its desire is for you, but you should rule over it.'" (Genesis 4:6–7)

God says plainly: "If you do well, will you not be accepted?" Yet verse 5 says God did not accept his offering or him. What does that tell us? Cain was not doing well. God makes it clear: just live the way you are supposed to live, and I will accept you. But Cain was upset rather than repentant.

Hebrews 11:4 adds: "By faith Abel offered to God a more excellent sacrifice than Cain." There was something significant about Abel's sacrifice—something different. But the real question is why Cain's offerings were not accepted.

The answer is that it had nothing to do with the offering itself. The excellence of the sacrifice really had more to do with the person bringing it. Proverbs 15:8 says: "The sacrifice of the wicked is an abomination to the LORD, but the prayer of the upright is His delight." The wicked can bring God anything of any value, and it will be worthless if they are a wicked person. But the righteous can simply lift up a prayer, and that is precious in God's sight. It is not about bringing God something of great value—it is about walking with the Lord.

Consider that Adam and Eve sinned in Genesis 3, and God clothed them with animal skins. Those animals had to die for God to get their skins—the first deaths on earth. God slew the animals, and through that death a covering was provided. Here begins the beautiful picture of sacrifice and covering. The Hebrew word kapur means "covering," but it is also translated "atonement." Their sins were covered through the death of an animal.

Adam would have continued bringing these sacrifices to the Lord, because Abel had to learn it from somewhere. Adam probably continued the pattern he saw when God sacrificed an animal. In Jude, we read about "the way of Cain"—the idea that Cain had a way about him. He did not want to do things the way God had prescribed. He wanted to do it his way, to give God what he thought he ought to give. It was selfish and self-centered. Cain wanted to worship God on his own terms.

That attitude exists in the church today—people who want to do things their way and bristle when they are told otherwise. If the Bible has spoken clearly, we should conform to the Bible. Cain wanted to worship God his way, on his terms.

Now something fascinating: in the Greek of 1 John 3, the word for "murdered" is *sphazō* (σφάζω), meaning to slay or kill. But it is specifically the word for ritual sacrifice— where an animal's throat would be slit. While we cannot be dogmatic about it, a good argument can be made that this is probably how Cain killed Abel. It is a unique word, used for the ritual sacrifice where the animal was held and its throat was slit before the altar.

Consider that Cain may never have seen anything else killed before, at least not by human hands. Meat did not become food until after the flood in Noah's time. The only things mankind was killing were the sheep they sacrificed and then used for wool and skins.

127

Imagine the scene: Cain is angry. God does not like his grain offering. For what it is worth, grain offerings were prescribed by God later in the Law, so it was not that God would never receive a grain offering. But at this point, He wanted a blood sacrifice. Cain is furious—"God likes Abel's sacrifice but not mine? I'll show Abel. I'll make Abel my sacrifice." And he probably slit his brother's throat.

Cain was of the wicked one. We are either sons of God or sons of the devil. That is why these thoughts came into Cain's mind—he had given his heart over to Satan. He was upset because his works were evil and his brother's were righteous. Why did God not accept Cain? Simply because Cain's works were not righteous. And his unrighteousness manifested itself in his behavior—ultimately, in the murder of his own brother.

The Assurance of Love
1 John 3:13-24

The World's Hatred

"Do not marvel, my brethren, if the world hates you." (1 John 3:13)

This raises an honest question: does the world hate us? Certainly there are many today who do not like Christians. But in the reality of it, believers are fairly accepted by many, especially in America. This raises the question: could we be doing better at being hated by the world?

Now, love does not behave rudely—that is clear from Scripture. We are not trying to be weird, nor are we ever trying to be hated. That is not the goal. But the world hated Christ. If we are trying to be like Christ and succeeding, we should expect to rub people the wrong way from time to time. We should expect that there is a potency to our lives that makes sinners uncomfortable in their sin.

There is a tactful way to continually be salt and light. Salt stings when put on a wound, and we need to be salty. Light exposes darkness, and we should be doing that—but in a loving way, in a tactful way, in what we believe to be the most edifying way.

Some take it to an extreme, blasting people with a full broadside of truth. But that does not help—it just makes people angry without making them hate us for being like Jesus. On the other hand, ignoring sin is not the solution either. If anything, the majority of the church today is a bit timid, worried about offending, worried about pushing people away.

But look at Jesus—He was forward about everything. How did He get away with it? Because He sincerely loved every person He was forward with. One of the greatest evangelists of our time, Ray Comfort, exemplifies this. He goes for the jugular when it comes to sin—telling people plainly that they are sinners heading for hell. Yet at the same time, he genuinely seems to care. When you hear him talking with people, he really does seem to love them. As long as we genuinely care about people, they will notice that. But they will not be happy if we bring up sin and its consequences and what happens if they do not turn to Jesus.

So do not marvel if the world hates you.

Passing from Death to Life

> *"We know that we have passed from death to life, because we love the brethren. He who does not love his brother abides in death. Whoever hates his brother is a murderer, and you know that no murderer has eternal life abiding in him."*
> (1 John 3:14–15)

A great way to know you are born again is your love for others in the church—or at bare minimum, knowing that you ought to love them. There may be people easier to love than others, but believers know they are supposed to love their brothers and sisters. Unbelievers feel no such obligation. They love the people who love them, the people who are nice to them. Jesus said, "Even tax collectors do that. To love those who love you is not a big deal." But Christians know we ought to love all people. As this conviction becomes reality and practice, we can have assurance that we have passed from death to life.

One of John's main purposes in this letter is assurance of salvation: "I have written that you may know you have eternal life." The phrase "passing from death to life" shows up in more than one place in the New Testament, but there is never a verse about passing from spiritual life to spiritual death—it simply does not exist. The Bible talks about being born again but never about being "dead again." It talks about passing from death to life but never life to death. These are important things to consider in discussions about eternal security. We have passed from death to life; we have eternal life currently in our possession.

Verse 15 says whoever hates his brother is a murderer. Either a person has eternal life abiding and remaining in them continually, or they do not have eternal life at all. One way to know is if hatred is present. This does not say "angry at" or "frustrated with"—hatred is a strong term. Hatred is the root of murder. People do not murder those they do not hate. If there is hatred in the heart, it will eventually manifest as something destructive.

Jesus made this connection in the Sermon on the Mount:

> *"You have heard that it was said to those of old, 'You shall not commit adultery.' But I say to you that whoever looks at a woman to lust for her has already committed adultery with her in his heart."* (Matthew 5:27–28)

It is the same concept with a different sin. God goes beyond actions and looks at the heart. If someone is lusting in their heart, they are simply missing the opportunity to commit adultery. If someone is hating in their heart, they are just missing the opportunity—perhaps just afraid of the consequences of murder. But if they could get away with it, they probably would.

Hatred is not becoming of a Christian. That is hard to hear because some people have been hurt in terrible ways. It can be difficult not to hate someone who has done something awful to you or someone you love. But only Christians do things like forgive murderers in courtrooms. A parent forgiving the person who killed their child, asking that person to receive Jesus—that is the work of God in a person's life, even through the hardest things and deepest pain. We might fight it, but deep down God will convict our hearts: we know what we need to do. We need to love even those who have wronged us, as God has called us to love.

Laying Down Our Lives

"By this we know love, because He laid down His life for us. And we also ought to lay down our lives for the brethren."
(1 John 3:16)

John 3:16 and 1 John 3:16 pair together beautifully. "For God so loved the world that He gave His only begotten Son"—and here, "By this we know love, because He laid down His life for us." When we speak of agape love as sacrificial, as love that comes at a cost, this is the verse to turn to. We understand what agape love is as we watch Christ lay down His life for us. It was a sacrifice.

Because we are trying to be imitators of Christ and become like our Father in heaven, we also ought to lay down our lives for the brethren. This is something we should be doing all the time, day after day.

Romans 12:10 captures this: "Be kindly affectionate to one another with brotherly love, in honor giving preference to one another." Laying down one's life is, in practice, giving preference to others. "I honor you, so I am choosing to lay down my preferences and choices to give you preference and choice."

A wonderful synergy takes place in a marriage, in a church, in any fellowship when people have this heart—the mind that was in Christ Jesus. He laid down His life; He emptied Himself to come in the likeness of man and sinful flesh. We too lay down our lives and empty ourselves of pride and preference for one another. When everyone is doing that—giving to each other—everyone is also receiving at the same time. It creates a beautiful dynamic.

Loving in Deed

> *"But whoever has this world's goods, and sees his brother in need, and shuts up his heart from him—how does the love of God abide in him? My little children, let us not love in word or in tongue, but in deed and in truth."* (1 John 3:17–18)

The phrase "whoever has this world's goods" does not mean whoever has an abundance of goods. Pretty much every commentary makes the same point: this refers to anyone who has anything. Having resources—not necessarily a lot, not necessarily extra—is the only prerequisite. It is not really a sacrifice when giving out of abundance, but we are called to lay down our lives for one another.

In Mark 12, Jesus pointed out the widow who gave her two mites:

> *"Assuredly, I say to you that this poor widow has put in more than all those who have given to the treasury; for they all put in out of their abundance, but she out of her*

133

> *poverty put in all that she had, her whole livelihood.* " (Mark 12:43–44)

This is the idea of measuring a gift by its cost. The greatest gift on earth is salvation, and the cost was God's only Son. When we give to one another, it should cost us something. This does not mean we should wait until we have "enough" before we start giving. Be generous now and have an intention to remain generous and become more generous.

There is wisdom in this, too. Dave Ramsey often says, "Live like no one else, so that one day you can live like no one else." It is good wisdom for Christians to make sacrifices now so they can set themselves up later to be even more generous. That saying has two sides: having financial peace and also giving like no one else. Getting to a place where one can give more freely is a worthy goal.

Starting out in marriage with humble beginnings, on a shoestring budget with couponing systems and binders just to get by month to month, the plan was to reach a place where that would no longer be necessary—and then to reach another place of even greater generosity, and then another. God blesses that when it is the genuine desire of the heart. But the key is not to wait. Do not say, "Someday, once I hit a certain milestone, I'll become generous." Be generous now. Give time, attention, and earthly things.

The other part of verse 17 is about shutting up the heart. If someone is shutting up their heart, there is a problem. If the heart is doing well and wisdom says "not now," that is different. If the heart is well and there truly are no goods to give, that is different. But do not shut up the heart.

Verse 18 is straightforward: "Let us not love in word or in tongue, but in deed and in truth." Talk is cheap. Telling someone "I love you" is easy—the deed and truth part takes effort. Actions must line up with words through acts of service and sacrifice. We need not just to tell people we love them, but to show them. Not "go in peace and be filled," but actually, practically showing love.

Assurance Before God

> *"And by this we know that we are of the truth, and shall assure our hearts before Him. For if our heart condemns us, God is greater than our heart, and knows all things. Beloved, if our heart does not condemn us, we have confidence toward God."*
> (1 John 3:19–21)

Here we find one of the most comforting truths in this letter. Before examining it, a small textual note is worth mentioning. The New Testament manuscripts were written in all capital letters, without punctuation, and even without spaces between words. This was common in that time. Hebrew had no vowels—readers knew the difference between words by context. Greek readers could read without spaces or punctuation just fine.

But when translating into English, where we depend on these things, translators sometimes have to make decisions. The Greek verbs and word forms implied certain breaks and connections, but occasionally the punctuation can be reworked for better flow. In verses 18–20, if we adjust the punctuation slightly, the passage has even better continuity.

Consider reading it this way: "My little children, let us not love in word or in tongue, but in deed and in truth, and by this we know we are of the truth." That forms one complete thought. Then: "And this shall assure our hearts before Him—that if our heart condemns us, God is greater than our heart, and knows all things."

135

John is saying: do not just talk the talk; walk the walk. Let us love in deed and in truth. As we walk out our faith, we will know we are of the truth—it will assure us. And here is another assurance: even if your heart condemns you, God is greater than your heart.

The heart might give a verdict of guilty, but that verdict can be taken to a higher court where God says, "No, you are not condemned." This is a wonderful promise. If we are faithless, He remains faithful. If our heart condemns us, that is okay because God is greater than our hearts and He knows better. If Satan has deceived someone in the moment, causing them to question and worry, they need not fear—God really knows the truth.

There is a story of a men's retreat where the speaker asked, "Raise your hand if you are just sold out for God and absolutely love the Lord." Almost no one raised their hand because people started thinking, "Am I really sold out? That's a heavy statement." Then the speaker stopped everyone: "No, no—at the end of the day, do you really know you love Him? You might fail in practice, but deep down you know you have a heart for God?" Everyone agreed. "Then raise your hand."

Our hearts condemn us so often. We feel like failures. But deep down, we know the truth. We know where our hearts truly lie. And if our hearts condemn us, God is greater than our hearts—which are wicked and deceitful—and He knows all things. He knows the real truth.

This should be both comforting and sobering. Nothing can be hidden from Him, and no fakers will get into heaven. But all who struggle and fight and claw tooth and nail— God knows the truth, and they do not need to worry when they are struggling.

John MacArthur put it well: "Security is a fact. Assurance is a gift." Studying the Bible reveals that believers are secure—that is a biblical fact. But we do not always feel that way. Having the peace of God that surpasses understanding is a gift. Having total assurance before God is a wonderful thing, and it is a gift. John is saying that if we do these things he describes, we will assure our hearts before Him.

Verse 21 takes it further: "Beloved, if our heart does not condemn us, we have confidence toward God." Even better than knowing God is greater than a condemning heart is when our heart does not condemn us at all—because we are walking in the truth. That just feels so much better. There is confidence that comes from making good choices, living for the Lord, forsaking evil and pursuing good.

Security is a fact, but assurance is a gift. Why ruin that assurance by playing around with sin? The Bible says sin is pleasurable for the moment, but it is passing—it goes away and leaves a person feeling like garbage in the end. Do not mess around with it. Be free, have great confidence before God, and walk in power.

Answered Prayer and Obedience

> *"And whatever we ask we receive from Him, because we keep His commandments and do those things that are pleasing in His sight. And this is His commandment: that we should believe on the name of His Son Jesus Christ and love one another, as He gave us commandment."* (1 John 3:22–23)

There is more blessing in obedience. What John describes is a state of being where a person is walking in truth, walking in victory, having confidence in God, enjoying communion with God—things are going well in their walk. Therefore, as they pray, they are praying the will of God and watching that will work out in their lives. Even when prayers do not go as expected, there is great assurance that God is in control—and that is all they ever wanted in the first place: God's will to be done, Him in control. So in a sense, all prayers are being answered.

Things go well when we do what is pleasing in His sight. There is a blessing to obedience, a blessing that comes with walking in the light.

Then John tells us what His commandment is. Some people in John's day—and in Paul's day—were trying to get Gentiles to "keep the commandments," meaning all the old ceremonial law. John cuts through that: "This is His commandment: believe on the name of His Son Jesus Christ and love one another."

That sounds straightforward. Want to keep His commandments? Believe on the Lord Jesus and love one another.

Notice that "commandment" is singular, yet John gives two things. First John is full of such paradoxes—one commandment, two commands. But the reality is that believing on the Lord Jesus and loving His children go together as a package deal. No one can truly believe on Him and then hate and mistreat their brothers and sisters. Something would not be adding up. So it is one commandment: when you love God, you will love His children. When you love someone, you will love their children too.

The phrase "believe on the name of His Son Jesus Christ" is important. Some translations say "believe in," but "believe on" captures something essential. Even the

demons believe and tremble. People believe in the tooth
fairy. Believing in something can simply mean believing it
exists. But believing on means placing oneself upon it,
trusting in its ability to sustain weight.

Believing on the Lord Jesus means resting upon Him, with
all weight placed there, fully expecting Him to carry us
home. That is saving faith.

The Spirit as Assurance

> *"Now he who keeps His commandments*
> *abides in Him, and He in him. And by this*
> *we know that He abides in us, by the Spirit*
> *whom He has given us."* (1 John 3:24)

This verse probably belongs thematically with chapter 4, as
First John's chapter divisions are slightly off in several
places. But it provides one last word on assurance: we
know He abides in us by the Spirit He has given us.

It is mutual—He abides in us, and we abide in Him. This
back-and-forth relationship is confirmed by the Spirit's
presence. Ephesians 1:13–14 explains:

> *"In Him you also trusted, after you heard*
> *the word of truth, the gospel of your*
> *salvation; in whom also, having believed,*
> *you were sealed with the Holy Spirit of*
> *promise, who is the guarantee of our*
> *inheritance until the redemption of the*
> *purchased possession, to the praise of His*
> *glory."* (Ephesians 1:13–14)

Every believer is sealed by the Holy Spirit. After hearing
the gospel and believing, believers are sealed up until God
gets to possess what He has purchased. The Holy Spirit is

given as an assurance, a guarantee. He seals believers to confirm that God is going to finish the work He started.

An important distinction should be made: being sealed is not the same as being filled. Churches see this differently, but going through the New Testament reveals people becoming believers and then later being filled with the Holy Spirit—the Spirit coming upon them in a distinct way.

Jesus breathed on the disciples and said, "Receive the Holy Spirit." Then He told them to wait in Jerusalem because the Spirit would come upon them. In Acts 19, Paul asked disciples at Ephesus, "Did you receive the Holy Spirit when you believed?"—or as the King James renders it, "Have you received the Holy Ghost since you believed?" Either way, the question implies a possibility of something beyond the initial sealing.

Believers are sealed forever but filled periodically. A Spirit-filled Christian is not a title; it is a condition. Conditions change over time. Throughout Acts, Peter is filled more than once—it is the verb "to fill up," not a permanent description but a repeated experience. We need those continual fillings of the Holy Spirit.

The great question then is: how full are we? We are sealed by the Holy Spirit—nothing changes that. But receiving the filling of the Holy Spirit, walking in obedience, is another matter. A quick way to drain the Spirit's filling is to walk in disobedience.

The Holy Spirit is pictured as a dove. When Noah sent the dove from the ark, it flew around and came back because it found no place to land. But before the dove, what did he send? A raven. The raven did not come back because there was dead stuff, carrion—ravens are happy to land on filth. Not the dove. It wants to find something clean to land on.

Walking in disobedience—whether drugs and immorality
or anger, greed, envy, pride—drives away the Spirit's
filling. We want to be clean vessels. We want assurance.
And there is no better way to have that assurance than
when we are obeying His commandments, loving Him, and
loving one another. Obeying what He says brings great
assurance and peace, and creates opportunity for the Holy
Spirit to come and do whatever He desires in our lives.

The Epistles of John

Testing the Spirits
1 John 3:24-4:15

Introduction: The Transition from Spirit to Spirits

First John is a book where the chapter breaks seem consistently off by a verse or two. Chapter one flows naturally into chapter two, the last two verses of chapter two really belong with chapter three, and here in chapter four, the content connects directly back to the final verse of chapter three. Understanding this literary flow helps illuminate John's argument.

In 1 John 3:24, John writes: *Now he who keeps His commandments abides in Him, and He in him. And by this we know that He abides in us, by the Spirit whom He has given us.*

The Spirit mentioned here is clearly the Holy Spirit—basic Christian teaching. But then in verse one of chapter four, John pivots with an urgent warning: do not believe every spirit. This transition requires some clarification about what John means by the word "spirit."

Understanding 'Spirit' in Scripture

The word "spirit" carries multiple meanings in Scripture. There is the human spirit—we are body, soul, and spirit. There is the Spirit of God, the Holy Spirit. Angelic beings are often called spirits, both good and evil, with demons being fallen angelic beings. And then there is another usage: the spirit of an age, or someone having an evil spirit in the sense of temperament or disposition rather than demonic possession.

Some teachers speak of a "spirit of lust" or a "spirit of drunkenness" as though demons are one-trick ponies, each limited to a single form of temptation. But Scripture does not support this view. Demons are not so specialized that one must "call cousin Vinnie, the spirit of drunkenness" to tempt someone to drink. Such teaching is simply not biblical.

In this passage, John addresses the spirit behind false teachers versus the Spirit behind true teachers of God. He speaks of the "spirit of antichrist"—which carries a twofold meaning: both a disposition that is like-minded with what we would expect from the Antichrist, and something that has genuine demonic origin and influence. It is not necessarily one specific demon named "the spirit of antichrist," but rather refers to teaching that carries the disposition and demonic influence opposed to Christ.

The Command to Stop Believing Every Spirit

> *Beloved, do not believe every spirit, but test the spirits, whether they are of God; because many false prophets have gone out into the world. (1 John 4:1)*

In the Greek, this command carries a present tense construction that, when paired with a negative, means more than simply "don't do this." It literally means "stop believing every spirit." John is addressing a problem already occurring among his readers. They had been too credulous, too willing to accept whatever teaching came their way.

The early church was prone to fall into false teaching. This vulnerability explains the numerous exhortations throughout the New Testament—to Timothy, to Titus, and to others—urging them to hold fast to the Word of God and test all teaching. Believers are to compare what they hear with Scripture, examining both the content and the character of those speaking.

Sheep are not known for their discernment. The imagery of sheep following shepherds captures an uncomfortable truth: sheep will follow anyone who has food, even a bad shepherd. John's warning—"stop believing every spirit"—addresses this tendency to trust whatever sounds appealing.

The Berean Example

The Bereans were considered more noble than the Thessalonians precisely because they did not simply accept Paul's teaching at face value. Acts 17 records that they searched the Scriptures daily to determine whether the things Paul said were true. Even an apostle's teaching was tested against Scripture. This is the model John commends.

Paul's Warning to the Corinthians

Second Corinthians 11:3–4 provides two critical verses on this matter of false doctrine: *But I fear, lest somehow, as the serpent deceived Eve by his craftiness, so your minds may be corrupted from the simplicity that is in Christ. For if he who comes preaches another Jesus whom we have not preached, or if you receive a different spirit which you have not received, or a different gospel which you have not accepted—you may well put up with it!*

Notice Paul's use of the Greek word heteros here—meaning "another of a different kind," as in heterosexual, being

145

attracted to someone of a different kind. This is distinguished from allos, which means "another of the same kind." Paul is not describing merely an alternative teaching but a fundamentally different gospel, a different spirit, a different Jesus—not what the apostles had preached.

Paul expresses the same alarm in Galatians 1:6–9: *I marvel that you are turning away so soon from Him who called you in the grace of Christ, to a different gospel, which is not another; but there are some who trouble you and want to pervert the gospel of Christ. But even if we, or an angel from heaven, preach any other gospel to you than what we have preached to you, let him be accursed. As we have said before, so now I say again, if anyone preaches any other gospel to you than what you have received, let him be accursed.*

Paul lays it out plainly: if someone preaches another Jesus, a different gospel, a different God—that person is anathema, accursed, headed for damnation. They do not believe in the correct Jesus. It cannot be merely a figure with the same name; it must be the same Person.

John's Immediate Context: Cerinthus the Heretic

John had a specific false teacher in mind when he wrote these words. Enter again, Cerinthus, the Gnostic contemporary of John in Ephesus. Irenaeus, who was a disciple of Polycarp (who was himself a disciple of John), preserved a remarkable story about John's encounter with this heretic.

According to Irenaeus, John once entered a bathhouse in Ephesus and discovered that Cerinthus was inside. John immediately fled, crying out: "Let us fly, lest even the bathhouse fall down on us, because Cerinthus, the enemy of truth, is inside!" John would not remain in the same building with this false teacher, fearing that God might bring judgment on the structure itself.

Again, Cerinthus taught that Jesus was merely a man upon whom the Spirit of Christ—the Spirit of Messiah—descended at His baptism. According to this teaching, God worked through Jesus until sometime before the crucifixion (likely at the Garden of Gethsemane), at which point the Spirit departed because, Cerinthus argued, the divine Spirit could not be killed. Thus Jesus died as a mere man.

This heresy directly attacked the incarnation. It denied that the eternal Son of God took on human flesh. It made Jesus merely a spirit-empowered prophet rather than God incarnate.

The Test: Confessing Jesus Christ Has Come in the Flesh

> *By this you know the Spirit of God: Every spirit that confesses that Jesus Christ has come in the flesh is of God, and every spirit that does not confess that Jesus Christ has come in the flesh is not of God. And this is the spirit of the Antichrist, which you have heard was coming, and is now already in the world. (1 John 4:2–3)*

John provides a doctrinal test rooted in the person of Christ. The key phrase is "Jesus Christ has come in the flesh." This confesses that Jesus—the eternal Son—came down from heaven and took on human nature. It aligns with Jesus's own teaching in John 6, where He declared Himself to be the bread that came down from heaven: "I was in heaven with the Father, and then I came down from heaven."

147

The direct teaching of Scripture is clear: Jesus pre-existed in heaven with the Father, and He came down from heaven in the flesh. Not that He was merely a man upon whom a spirit descended, but that the eternal Son Himself took on human nature. This is what Cerinthus denied, and this is what John's test addresses.

A True Test, But Not the Only Test

An important clarification is necessary here. This is a true test, but it is not the only test for identifying false teaching. Some Christians have suggested that anyone who affirms "Jesus came in the flesh" should be accepted as orthodox. But John was providing one specific test that directly addressed the heresy plaguing his congregation.

There are many other forms of false teaching. The two essentials that typically distinguish a church from a cult, a saving gospel from a false gospel, are the nature of God and the nature of salvation. Who is God? If someone believes in a fundamentally different God, they are outside the faith. What is the gospel? Salvation by faith in Jesus alone, or faith plus something else?

Many want to minimize these distinctions, but they are serious matters. We are saved by faith in Jesus. When teachers begin adding requirements to that—the gospel plus works, the gospel plus baptism, the gospel plus confirmation, the gospel plus church attendance—they pervert the true gospel. All these good things ought to flow from salvation, but they cannot be added to the gospel as requirements for salvation.

John himself makes this point elsewhere in his letter: loving people does not save us, but saved people love. The order matters. We cannot love our way into heaven, but if we are saved, love should characterize our lives.

The Spirit of Antichrist

John identifies false teaching that denies Christ's incarnation as "the spirit of the Antichrist." His readers knew that the Antichrist was coming, but John reveals that the spirit behind the Antichrist—Satan himself—was already at work in the world through false teachers.

As John MacArthur has observed, all spiritual truth either comes from a divine source or a demonic source. Every false religion, however attractive it may appear, ultimately has its origin in Satan. This is a remarkably effective strategy for keeping people from the one true God: present them with alternative religions that appeal to their culture and preferences.

Excursus: Modern Groups Preaching a Different Jesus

While Cerinthus is long gone, his spirit lives on. Two groups that most commonly confront believers today preach a fundamentally different Jesus than the one revealed in Scripture. Because they believe in a different Jesus, they cannot rightly be called Christians, no matter how much they may use Christian vocabulary.

The Jehovah's Witnesses (Watchtower Society)

A key point to understand about Jehovah's Witnesses is that every piece of their official literature is considered inspired. Their publications—including the Watchtower magazine—carry the same authority as Scripture in their system. This means their official statements can be quoted as authoritative representations of their beliefs.

Regarding the nature of Jesus, Jehovah's Witness teaching states: *"This means that he was created before all other spirit sons of God and that he is the only one who is directly created by God."* According to their December 1981 Watchtower: *"Jesus is not almighty God. He is a created being, subordinate to Jehovah."*

The Watchtower further states: *"Jesus was not God incarnate. He was a perfect man who gave his life for mankind."* They explain the term "only begotten" this way: *"He is the only one directly created by Jehovah God. All other things came into existence through him as God's chief agent."*

In Jehovah's Witness theology, God created Jesus first, and then Jesus created everything else—hence "only begotten." This stands in direct contradiction to the biblical understanding of these terms.

When Scripture calls Jesus the "firstborn" in Colossians, it uses a term of preeminence, not chronological sequence. The firstborn son was the heir, the one who inherited all things. It was a title of honor and position, not a statement about birth order. And when Jesus is called the "only begotten Son," it speaks to His unique relationship with the Father. All believers are sons and daughters of God by adoption, but Jesus is the only begotten Son. When Jesus called God His Father, it upset the Jews because they understood the implication: if a dog has a son, it is a dog; if a parakeet has a son, it is a parakeet; and if God has a Son, He is God.

The Watchtower explicitly denies worship of Jesus: *"Though we love and deeply respect Jesus, we do not worship him. Worship belongs to Jehovah alone."*

Additionally, Jehovah's Witnesses teach that Jesus was originally the archangel Michael. Their literature states: "Scriptural evidence indicates the son of God was known as Michael before he came to Earth."

They also deny the bodily resurrection of Christ. According to the Watchtower: *"Jesus was resurrected not as a human creature but as a spirit. The man Jesus is dead, forever dead. God disposed of the human body. No one knows how."* (Interestingly, the founder Charles Taze Russell had earlier taught that Jesus's body was "dissolved into gases," representing an internal contradiction in their teachings.)

Finally, Jehovah's Witnesses teach that Jesus returned invisibly in 1914 and has been reigning in heaven ever since. After multiple failed predictions about Christ's return in the late 1800s and early 1900s, they eventually declared that He did return in 1914—it was simply an invisible, spiritual return. Their literature states: "Jesus's second presence began in 1914, and he has been ruling as king since then."

The Church of Jesus Christ of Latter-day Saints (Mormons)

The Mormon church teaches a different Jesus and a different God the Father as well. Their scriptures consist of the Book of Mormon, Doctrine and Covenants, and the Pearl of Great Price, often bound together with the King James Bible in what they call a "quad."

Joseph Smith taught concerning God the Father: *"If you were to see him today, you would see him like a man in form."* Yet Scripture declares that no one has seen God at any time (John 1:18), because God is spirit (John 4:24). We see Jesus Christ the Son; we do not see the Father.

Doctrine and Covenants 130:22 states: *"The Father has a body of flesh and bones as tangible as man's; the Son also; but the Holy Ghost has not a body of flesh and bones, but is a personage of spirit. Were it not so, the Holy Ghost could not dwell in us."*

Mormon theology teaches that Satan and all human beings are Jesus's spiritual younger siblings. Every person born on earth was first a spirit child of the Heavenly Father and one of his heavenly wives. Jesus was the firstborn of these spirit children.

Their teaching states: *"Every person who was born on earth was our spirit brother or sister in heaven. The firstborn to our heavenly parents was Jesus Christ. So, he is literally our elder brother."*

This is where the claim that Mormons believe Jesus and Satan are brothers originates. They actually believe everyone is spiritually related—Jesus is simply the eldest spirit child. The Doctrine and Covenants declares: "I was in the beginning with the Father, and am the Firstborn"— emphasizing Jesus as the firstborn spirit child, with Satan as the second born, followed by angels and eventually all humanity.

Regarding Jesus's conception, Mormon teaching holds that God the Father (whom they call "Heavenly Father") physically begot Jesus with Mary. This is why they say Jesus is "the only begotten." Their literature states: *"Jesus is the only person on earth to be born of a mortal mother and an immortal father."*

Brigham Young taught: *"When the virgin Mary conceived the child Jesus, the Father had begotten him in his own likeness. He was not begotten by the Holy Ghost. The man Joseph, the husband of Mary, did not... Who did? The*

Father of our Lord Jesus Christ. Jesus, our elder brother, was begotten in the flesh by the same character that was in the Garden of Eden, who was our father in heaven."

It should be noted that Brigham Young also taught the Adam-God doctrine—that Adam became God the Father after his death. While later Mormon presidents have distanced themselves from this teaching, it remains part of their prophetic record, creating internal inconsistencies within their tradition.

Bruce McConkie wrote in Mormon Doctrine: *"Christ was begotten by an immortal Father in the same way mortal men are begotten by mortal fathers."*

Perhaps the clearest statement of Mormon theology comes from their fifth president, Lorenzo Snow, who declared: "As man is, God once was; and as God is, man may become." Every informed Mormon knows this phrase. It means that God in heaven was once a human being just like us, and if Mormons are faithful, they too can achieve godhood.

This directly contradicts the God of the Bible. Isaiah chapters 40-48 repeatedly declare that there is no God before Him, no God beside Him, and no God after Him. He alone is God from everlasting to everlasting.

The Pearl of Great Price even specifies that God lives near a star called Kolob. It describes the origin of Satan: *"Satan, whom thou hast commanded in the name of thine only begotten, is the same which was from the beginning, and he came before me, saying, 'Behold, here I am, send me, I will be thy son, and I will redeem all mankind, that one soul should not be lost.'"*

According to Mormon teaching, when God needed to formulate a plan of salvation, both Jesus and Satan

153

proposed plans. The Father chose Jesus's plan, and Satan has been in rebellion ever since.

Finally, Mormons teach that Jesus attained His divine status. Doctrine and Covenants 93:13-14 states: *"Jesus received not the fullness at the first, but continued from grace to grace, until he received a fullness."* In other words, Jesus earned His godhood through a perfect life— the same path Mormons believe is open to them.

The Importance of Testing

Many believers know generally that Mormons and Jehovah's Witnesses have serious doctrinal problems. But there is an overwhelming amount of false teaching available today—on YouTube, in books, across the internet. I have personally watched people leave solid, Bible-teaching churches and fall into the exact same heresies and cults that the apostle Paul was warning against in the first century.

The Hebrew Roots movement, for instance, is essentially the Judaizing heresy that Paul addressed in half his letters—people trying to bring Christians back under the Mosaic Law. Yet it continues to draw people away from the truth.

We must test everything according to Scripture. Some groups teach a completely different Jesus and a completely different gospel—these are clearly outside the faith. Other groups exist on the fringe: they may have added prophets, extra-biblical teachings, and various strange beliefs, yet still affirm the same Jesus and essentially the same gospel. Discernment requires recognizing that someone might be a genuine believer in an unhealthy environment, while also identifying what clearly separates a cult from the church.

Greater Is He Who Is in You

*You are of God, little children, and have
overcome them, because He who is in you is
greater than he who is in the world. They
are of the world. Therefore they speak as of
the world, and the world hears them. We are
of God. He who knows God hears us; he
who is not of God does not hear us. By this
we know the spirit of truth and the spirit of
error. (1 John 4:4–6)*

After this sobering warning about false teachers, John
offers tremendous encouragement. His readers have
nothing to fear from these false prophets because they have
overcome them. How? Because He who is in them—the
Holy Spirit—is greater than he who is in the world—Satan
and his demonic forces.

When believers are abiding in the love of God and walking
in the Holy Spirit, they need not fear being deceived.
Deception typically comes when we are caught up in our
flesh, pursuing our own ideas and desires. But the Spirit
provides discernment to those who walk with Him.

Worldly Speech Attracts Worldly Hearers

Verse five reveals why false teaching often gains a
following: false teachers speak as of the world, and the
world hears them. Their message resonates with worldly
thinking because it originates there. But believers are not of
the world, so this worldly message should not appeal to
them.

People may profess to believe in God and love God, but
their speech often reveals their true spiritual condition. Let
someone speak candidly outside the church for a while, and

155

much can be revealed by what comes out of their mouth. As Jesus taught, out of the abundance of the heart the mouth speaks. When someone's regular conversation does not sound like someone in whom the Holy Spirit dwells, that is cause for concern.

The old saying applies: "Better to keep your mouth closed and have people think you're a fool than to open it and prove it." What proceeds from our mouths reveals the thoughts and intents of our hearts.

The Apostolic 'We'

In verse six, John shifts his language in a way that can be confusing. Sometimes in this letter he uses "we" to include all believers—"we're in this together." But at other points he uses "we" to refer specifically to the apostles. This appears to be one of those instances.

"We are of God"—that is, we the apostles are of God, not the false teachers. "He who knows God hears us; he who is not of God does not hear us." John is asserting apostolic authority: those who truly know God will receive apostolic teaching; those who reject apostolic teaching demonstrate that they do not know God.

When someone refuses to hear the Word of God—not merely sitting through a sermon, but actually receiving correction from Scripture when confronted about sin in their life—it often reveals their spiritual condition. If the general pattern of someone's life is "I don't care what the Bible says," that person is likely spiritually dead. The things of God will not make sense to them because spiritual truths must be spiritually discerned, and that requires the Holy Spirit.

Believers, even immature ones in seasons of rebellion, will ultimately receive the Word of God gladly. They are willing to be corrected by Scripture. When someone consistently rejects the Bible, they have rejected God. It is plain and simple.

Love: The Mark of Those Born of God

Beloved, let us love one another, for love is of God; and everyone who loves is born of God and knows God. He who does not love does not know God, for God is love.
(1 John 4:7–8)

Having addressed the danger of false spirits, John returns to his major theme: love. The transition is significant. The way to recognize true believers is not merely by doctrinal confession (though that matters), but by the fruit of love in their lives.

In verse seven, the Greek text includes a definite article before "love" that is not always translated into English. The phrase could be rendered: "Beloved, let us love one another, for *this* love is of God." John is emphasizing a specific kind of love—not worldly love, not sensual love, not merely natural family affection, but a love that originates in God.

This is the agape love that 1 Corinthians 13 describes. It is the love with which God so loved the world that He gave His only begotten Son. It is a special kind of love that comes from God and reflects His character. Everyone who loves with this agape love is born of God and knows God. True selfless, sacrificial love can only flow from those who have been born again.

The order is critical: loving a lot will not get anyone into heaven. Loving cannot earn salvation. But knowing God produces love. The relationship with God comes first; love is the fruit. John states it plainly: "He who does not love does not know God, for God is love."

This provides a diagnostic for observers. When we see people who are loveless—selfish rather than selfless—we can recognize that something is spiritually wrong. All believers struggle with selfishness to some degree, but love should define the Christian church. Love should characterize God's people.

The Manifestation of God's Love

In this the love of God was manifested toward us, that God has sent His only begotten Son into the world, that we might live through Him. In this is love, not that we loved God, but that He loved us and sent His Son to be the propitiation for our sins. (1 John 4:9–10)

Here is how we understand and see God's love: He sent His only begotten Son into the world. Again, John emphasizes against Cerinthus's heresy: the Spirit did not merely come upon a man named Jesus—God sent His Son into the world. Jesus has come in the flesh that we might live through Him.

That phrase is significant: "that we might live through Him." God does not merely want us to live better; He wants us to live through Christ, empowered by Him, accomplishing what He empowers us to accomplish in the way He empowers us to do it. The Christian life is not self-improvement but Christ living through us.

I have had opportunity to counsel believers struggling with doubt and worry. Two foundational truths provide anchor points. First, remember that God loves you. Whenever doubt or worry assaults, filter every thought through this reality: the almighty God of the universe loves me in such a way that He sent His Son to die for me. What else would He withhold? As Paul writes in Romans 8:32, "He who did not spare His own Son, but delivered Him up for us all, how shall He not with Him also freely give us all things?" If God would give Jesus, why would He not give us anything else that is good for us and part of His plan?

Second, when uncertain about what to do or how to proceed, focus on loving God. If someone truly loves God, He will guide them. The Holy Spirit will direct their path if that is genuinely their heart's desire. This is not a blank check to live however one pleases—if someone lives any way they want, they do not truly love God. But as Augustine paraphrased: if you love God with all your heart, with all your soul, and with all your strength, then you can do whatever you want because you will only want to do the Father's will.

Psalm 37:4 promises that God will give us the desires of our heart—when our heart is fully His, He aligns our desires with His will. We receive everything we want because everything we want is what God has for us.

Not Our Love, But His

Verse ten contains a crucial clarification: "In this is love, not that we loved God, but that He loved us." God desires that we love Him in return, but that is not His chief concern. What matters most is that He loved us and sent His Son to be the propitiation for our sins.

159

More than how much we can love God, He is interested in how well we receive His love. Rather than focusing on what we can do for Him, He delights when we receive with an open heart what He has done for us. There is nothing we can do to repay Him. There is nothing we can offer that He does not already deserve.

Sometimes we fall into the temptation of bargaining with God: "Lord, if You do this, then I will do that." The Holy Spirit often convicts us immediately: "Should you not be doing that anyway?" We already owe God everything. We cannot make deals with Him. But the greatest gift we can give Him is receiving His gift to us. It is that simple.

Loving One Another as God's Children

Beloved, if God so loved us, we also ought to love one another. No one has seen God at any time. If we love one another, God abides in us, and His love has been perfected in us. (1 John 4:11–12)

If we want to bless God's heart, the best way to serve Him is by serving one another. Period. Any parent with multiple children understands this instinctively. If children could give their parents anything, it would be for them to simply love one another. When siblings are being kind to each other, playing together, the older ones caring for the younger—that warms a parent's heart. Children are sinners by nature, prone to bickering and conflict, but those moments when they genuinely love each other bring immense joy.

The same is true with our Heavenly Father. If God so loved us, we ought to love one another. If we want to make God happy, if we want to bless His heart, then we should love our brothers and sisters.

And let us define love once more: biblical agape love is sacrificial. It always costs something. There is no way to truly love another person without it costing us something—time, possessions, preferences. Romans 12 speaks of giving preference to one another with brotherly affection. Sometimes we must swallow our pride, eat crow, yield our rights. True love will cost us because we are pouring into others without expecting anything in return.

Phileo—brotherly affection—is meant to accompany agape. We need both. But agape especially requires sacrifice, pouring ourselves out for one another.

No One Has Seen God at Any Time

Verse twelve states that no one has seen God at any time. This is a biblical truth: God the Father has never been seen by human eyes. What about Moses? In Exodus, God placed Moses in a cleft of rock, covered him, and passed by so that Moses saw God's passing glory—like seeing the wake of a boat after it has passed. He did not see God directly.

What about the elders who dined on Mount Sinai and saw the throne of God, with the pavement under His feet like sapphire? They saw something glorious, but they did not see God Himself. Scripture speaks of God dwelling in unapproachable light. We may never fully see God the Father even in eternity—the glory radiating from that throne may always be too magnificent for our comprehension. Yet at His right hand is the Lamb of God, still bearing the marks of His crucifixion (Revelation 5). We will see Jesus face to face. Scripture makes that abundantly clear.

Who walked with Adam and Eve in the Garden? I believe it was Jesus. Who wrestled with Jacob at the Jabbok? I believe it was Jesus. The pre-incarnate Christ appeared

161

throughout the Old Testament, but God the Father remained unseen.

Seeing God Through His People

Why does John mention this here? Because he is making a profound point: when we love one another, God abides in us and His love is perfected in us. When God's love is manifested through His people, that is the way the world sees God.

This is why Jesus said they will know His disciples by their love. The best way to draw unbelievers to the gospel is for them to witness the love Christians have for one another. When the world sees a community where people genuinely sacrificially love each other, they see God. "God is in that church. How do you know? Look at how they love one another."

It was a significant realization for me when I understood that the New Testament's explicit commands to love are predominantly Christian to Christian, not generic love for all humanity. We are to love our neighbors and all people, certainly. But the emphasis falls on believers loving believers because that supernatural love displays God to a watching world.

Abiding Through the Spirit

By this we know that we abide in Him, and He in us, because He has given us of His Spirit. And we have seen and testify that the Father has sent the Son as Savior of the world. Whoever confesses that Jesus is the Son of God, God abides in him, and he in God. (1 John 4:13–15)

How do we know that we abide in God and He in us? Because He has given us His Spirit. The Holy Spirit is God in us, the spirit of love working through us. And the apostles—the "we" here likely refers again to the apostolic witness—have seen and testified that the Father sent the Son as Savior of the world.

That is what Jesus came to do. He came to be the Savior of the world. When He cried from the cross "It is finished," it was mission accomplished. The work of salvation was completed.

Verse fifteen returns to the doctrinal test: "Whoever confesses that Jesus is the Son of God, God abides in him, and he in God." John circles back to address Cerinthus once more. The false teacher denied that Jesus was truly the Son of God; he claimed Jesus was merely a man upon whom the Spirit temporarily rested. But confession that Jesus is the Son of God—truly God come in the flesh—marks genuine faith.

The Gnostic heresies attacked from both ends. Some, like Cerinthus, denied Christ's deity—Jesus was a man, not God. Others denied His humanity—Jesus was a spirit being who only appeared to have a body. Both are false. Jesus Christ is fully God and fully man, the eternal Son who took on human flesh.

Conclusion

John began this section with an urgent warning: stop believing every spirit. The early church was gullible, prone to follow any teacher with a compelling message. That danger has not diminished. Modern equivalents of Cerinthus abound—groups teaching a different Jesus, a different gospel, a different God.

The solution is threefold. First, test everything against Scripture. The Bereans provide the model: examine what you hear to see if it aligns with God's Word. Second, walk in the Spirit. Those who abide in Christ have nothing to fear from deception because He who is in them is greater than he who is in the world. Third, love one another sacrificially. This love marks genuine believers and makes God visible to a watching world.

Doctrinal truth and practical love are not competitors—they are companions. John moves seamlessly from warning about false teachers to emphasizing brotherly love because both matter. Sound doctrine about Christ guards against deception; love for one another demonstrates that we truly know the God of that doctrine.

As we will see in the following passage, these themes continue to interweave. But for now, let us take John's exhortations seriously: test the spirits, abide in Christ, and love one another. In doing so, we guard against error, experience God's presence, and display His character to those who have not yet seen Him.

Love Perfected
1 John 4:16-19

God loves you! Certainly, this is something believers know—but do they really know it? Have they forgotten it? Are they experiencing it? The walk of faith will begin and end with an understanding of the love of God.

In 1 John chapter 4, the apostle John mentions agape love twenty-seven times across just twenty-one verses. Love is the main subject. As Chuck Smith wisely observed, "All doctrinal orthodoxy and understanding of Scripture is of no value without love." This is a striking statement from a man who left behind a legacy of teaching the Bible and helping people understand Scripture. Yet all of that, as Paul puts it in 1 Corinthians 13, is like a clanging cymbal if we don't have love.

It cannot be this world's love—the kind of love seen on television or the kind of love that may have been experienced growing up, tainted or broken in some way. Believers must understand God's love. These four verses in 1 John 4:16–19 are packed full of valuable information, and each line deserves careful attention.

Known and Believed: The Love of God

> *"And we have known and believed the love that God has for us. God is love, and he who abides in love abides in God, and God in him."* (1 John 4:16)

Verse 16 begins with two different concepts: knowing and believing. Knowing has to do with understanding, while believing has to do with faith for things that are yet to come. The important word to focus on here is "known." There is more than one word in Greek for "to know." The word used here is *ginōskō* (γινώσκω), which is unique in meaning experiential knowledge. There is also *oida* (οἶδα), a Greek word that simply means to know. But *ginōskō* means to know something personally, intimately—to know it because of direct experience with it.

Consider the difference between saying, "I know who the president is," versus saying, "I have his number in my phone and we chat often." One is knowing about the man; the other is actually knowing the man. This is what John is talking about—experiential knowledge of God, where God has done something in a person's life such that they have experienced Him and therefore truly know Him.

I have asked people, "How many of you have ever been shocked by a spark plug wire on a car?" A handful will raise their hands. "How many have been shocked by household electricity?" A few more. Those who have experienced it know the feeling of being shocked—they have experiential knowledge of it. Others may understand intellectually that touching certain things will result in a painful shock, but they haven't felt it themselves. Having been shocked many times by both sources, I can say the feeling is unmistakable. To know the love of God is similar. There is a knowledge there that anyone who has experienced it recognizes as more than just intellectual understanding—it is experiential knowledge. "I have felt it. I know the feeling that God loves me and His love is inside of me."

This experiential knowledge then leads to believing, where faith can extend to things not yet seen. Christians do not have blind faith, though the world sometimes accuses believers of this. It works like seeing five feet of ice sticking out above the water on an iceberg—there is faith that a whole lot more ice is under the water because that's how icebergs work. It is the faith of watching someone do a trick on the trapeze a hundred times and trusting they'll do it again, because faithfulness has been demonstrated in the past. Because believers have experienced God, they can also have faith and believe in those things He has promised but which have not yet been seen.

The Love That Is In Us

The text says believers have "known and believed the love that God has for us." In the Greek, it literally reads "the love that he has in us," because He does have love for us—that is obvious. But more than that, believers have experienced something and understand there is a love inside of them.

> *"Now hope does not disappoint, because the love of God has been poured out in our hearts by the Holy Spirit who was given to us."* (Romans 5:5)

God is love. That is what the text says: "God is love, and he who abides in love abides in God, and God in him." God is love, and God abides in believers. Thus, if believers abide in His love, they are abiding in Him. If the Holy Spirit, who is God and therefore love, is living in a person, then the sign of that will be evident in their life.

The idea that God dwells inside of believers who is love should be evident to all. In fact, to call oneself a Christian and have others perceive them as an unloving person would be a frightful thing, because those two realities are absolutely contradictory.

Jesus emphasized this in His prayer before His arrest in the Garden of Gethsemane:

> *"...that the world may know that You have*
> *sent Me, and have loved them as You have*
> *loved Me."* (John 17:23)

This prayer in John 17 comes in sections. First, Jesus prays for Himself. Then He prays for the disciples. But this part is actually the tail end of the prayer—praying for those who will believe, which includes believers today. It is not just the twelve. Jesus prays, "I want them to know that You have loved them in the same manner that You have loved Me." God loves believers just as He loves Jesus.

To put it in terms that may hit closer to home: if someone has a son or daughter and has any feelings of love for that child, God loves them that way—but more. He loves with a perfect love.

> *"And I have declared to them Your name,*
> *and will declare it, that the love with which*
> *You loved Me may be in them, and I in*
> *them."* (John 17:26)

Jesus manifested the characteristics of God and who He was, so that the love with which the Father loves the Son may be in believers. There is this emphasis that if someone is a believer and born again, the love of God will be inside of them. It comes as a package deal. If a person has not experientially felt the love of God and that change in their life, that is not a good thing.

Christianity cannot become entirely about experiences—"I feel this" and "I experience that." The faith must be based on the Word of God. But the Word of God clearly does say that when someone becomes a believer, they are going to experience the love of God. Things are going to change. They will find desires for new things they didn't once have. They will find a hatred for things they used to enjoy.

Another thing that is natural to a believer—yes, believers get into funks, and there are difficult seasons—but when someone becomes a believer, they love other believers. It becomes normal. In fact, they want to go to church because they love the people at church.

About a decade ago, my wife and I moved down to Grand View to plant a church. Before that, for four years I drove every day from Ellensburg to Grand View and back—eighty miles each way. People would ask, "Why not just move to Grand View?" I only had one true answer: our church was in Ellensburg. That's where our family was. We didn't have a house when I first started the drive; later we bought one. But the reality was that our church was our family—the people we loved. When God's love is inside of us, these are natural things that take place.

But it does take time.

Love Perfected Among Us

> *"Love has been perfected among us in this:*
> *that we may have boldness in the day of*
> *judgment. Because as He is, so are we in*
> *this world."* (1 John 4:17)

Verse 17 says, "Love has been perfected among us in this." This is one place where the New King James does not translate as clearly as it might. The King James reads, "Herein is our love made perfect." The New Living Translation says, "And as we live in God, our love grows more perfect."

The idea is this: the King James "herein" is looking backward to verse 16. Believers have experienced God's love. They believe in God's love. Now God's love is abiding in them and they in Him. So "herein"—because of

169

God's love abiding in believers—their love is being made more perfect. Or as the NLT paraphrases it, as believers live in God and abide in Him from verse 16, their love is growing more perfect.

The Greek word for "perfected" is *teleioō* (τελειόω), which means to bring something to the end or goal that was intended. God has an intent to mature and grow believers in His love, and so they are being moved little by little toward that maturity.

When Jesus was dying on the cross, His second-to-last words were "It is finished"—*tetelestai* in the Greek, the verb form of this same word. It is finished. Paid in full. Done. He came to this world to save the world from sin, and at that very moment it was finished.

John is saying here that as believers abide in God and He in them, His love will be made more and more perfect, brought closer to that finished goal.

John Was Not Always the Apostle of Love

It is worth remembering that John himself was not always the "apostle of love." One pastor, Don McClure, has a dry humor that makes his sermons memorable. He points out that John the Apostle, who is known as the apostle of love and speaks about love more than anyone else in the New Testament, was once a very different man.

If we go back to when John was perhaps a teenager— eighteen or nineteen years old, as many scholars believe he was when he walked with Jesus—we find a striking incident. The disciples were trying to find a place to stay in Samaria, and the people would not let them stay there:

*"And when His disciples James and John
saw this, they said, 'Lord, do You want us to
command fire to come down from heaven
and consume them, just as Elijah did?'"*
(Luke 9:54)

Consider this: they were not talking about one man. They
were talking about an entire town. "Jesus, we should just
smoke the whole town. After that, everyone will listen.
We'll get free rooms and room upgrades. They'll know fire
could come at any moment."

The funny thing is that most people have thought evil
thoughts about someone in traffic—"If only I could..." But
such thoughts are silly because they could never actually
follow through. The difference with John is that Jesus
actually could have called down fire and literally destroyed
that entire town. So when John says this, he is not posing
some outlandish impossibility. He seems serious. "Elijah
did it. Let's send bears after them like Elisha did when they
called him bald."

John had a lot of growing to do in the area of love. Yet as
an old man, the early church fathers record that John, in his
nineties and frail, would be carried into the church service.
Still with a thunderous voice despite his old age, he would
only have the energy to tell the church, "Little children,
love one another."

When studying the book of Revelation, it becomes clear
that John wrote the seven letters to deliver to the seven
churches, and his church was the first one listed—Ephesus,
the church that had left its first love. So that became his
ongoing message: keep loving, keep loving, keep loving.

But it takes time for love to be perfected. Believers should
not expect to become Christians and suddenly become so
loving and happy that everyone receives them without

issue. They are going to grow in it. As they abide in Christ and He in them, the love of God will become perfected in them.

Boldness in the Day of Judgment

The telltale sign of Christian maturity is not Bible verses memorized or sins quit—it is growing in love. And verse 17 says that when the love of God is perfected in believers as they abide in God, watching and seeing themselves become more loving, "we may have boldness in the day of judgment."

> *"For we must all appear before the judgment seat of Christ, that each one may receive the things done in the body, according to what he has done, whether good or bad."* (2 Corinthians 5:10)

Every Christian will stand before the *bema* seat—that is the Greek word for judgment—to receive rewards for the things they have done. There is a sobering thought in standing before Jesus and having it all laid bare. But John is saying that if believers simply abide in love, work on abiding in Him who is love and letting His love abide in them, then they can have boldness in that day. They can say, "I have been loving. I am growing in love. Other people see the love of God in me. I have nothing to fear when I stand before the Lord."

The Puritan Richard Sibbes wrote, "The more we see the grace of God in Christ, the spirit of fear is diminished and replaced by a spirit of love and boldness." Once again, as believers experience God's grace and His love more and more, they have no reason to fear anymore. There is nothing to be afraid of because they have God inside of them, working in them.

As He Is, So Are We

Verse 17 continues: "Because as He is, so are we in this world."

This is a portion of Scripture that requires careful study, because sometimes verses in the Bible can be taken more than one way. Usually, comparing Scripture with Scripture clarifies meaning—if one interpretation contradicts other clear passages, it cannot be the correct meaning. This is rightly dividing the word of truth. But sometimes both possible interpretations are entirely scriptural.

One way to read this is: "As God is love, so we are to be in this world." That is certainly scriptural. But in the context of the previous phrase about having boldness in the day of judgment, there is another reading: "As Jesus is, so are we in this world."

> "...to the praise of the glory of His grace, by which He made us accepted in the Beloved."
> (Ephesians 1:6)

The Beloved is Jesus. Because of His grace, believers are accepted in Christ.

> "But God, who is rich in mercy, because of His great love with which He loved us, even when we were dead in trespasses, made us alive together with Christ (by grace you have been saved), and raised us up together, and made us sit together in the heavenly places in Christ Jesus." (Ephesians 2:4–6)

This is written in the present tense, yet looking around, believers do not appear to be sitting in the heavenly places. We try to keep our church buildings clean, but no one has ever walked in and said, "This place is so heavenly looking." It does not feel like sitting in the heavenly places.

So why does Paul write it this way? Because he was making the point that in God's eyes, because of Jesus, because of the Beloved, believers are accepted because of Him. As God sees believers in this world, He sees them as already sitting right there next to Jesus in heaven. Their spot is reserved. In God's eyes, it is as if they are already there because God is timeless. He is outside of time. In God's eyes right now, believers are already in heaven because He can experience all times at the same time. It is mind-blowing to consider.

Richard Sibbes wrote, "This is our comfort and our confidence, that God accepts us because He accepts His Beloved. God loves us with that inseparable love wherewith He loves His own Son."

John 17 already established this point—that Jesus prayed that future believers could know that God loves them just as He loves Jesus. When believers can understand that God sees them through Christ and in Christ, and it is all because of His love for them, it changes their own view of themselves. It changes a lot of things.

No Fear in Love

> *"There is no fear in love; but perfect love casts out fear, because fear involves torment. But he who fears has not been made perfect in love."* (1 John 4:18)

Verse 18 says, "There is no fear in love." If someone has only a little love, they might find there is still room for some fear. But the idea is that perfect love casts out fear. As love is perfected—this process as God's love is perfected in believers—it crowds out and eliminates the room where fear can be.

When speaking of fear, the Greek word *phobos* (φόβος), from which we get "phobia," can mean either terror or reverence, just as in English the word can have different meanings. This verse is not saying there should be no reverence in love. Consider these Old Testament passages:

> *"The fear of the LORD is clean, enduring forever."* (Psalm 19:9)

> *"The fear of the LORD is the beginning of wisdom."* (Psalm 111:10)

> *"The fear of the LORD is the beginning of knowledge."* (Proverbs 1:7)

> *"The fear of the LORD prolongs days."* (Proverbs 10:27)

> *"The fear of the LORD leads to life."* (Proverbs 19:23)

> *"The fear of the LORD is a fountain of life."* (Proverbs 14:27)

This is reverential fear—a good fear that love promotes.

If someone had a bad father, a wicked father, a man who did not raise them the way he should have, they could have been afraid of him if he had done awful things. But our Father is a good Father. And if someone has had a good father on this earth, they are going to fear him too—it is just a different kind of fear. It is reverence.

With a good father—the best dad imaginable—there is still fear. If that father set a nine o'clock curfew and his child came in at one in the morning, there is fear. And it is a good fear, because he loves them. God loves believers with a perfect love.

So when believers experientially know—*ginōskō*—who it is who loves them and how much He loves them, there is nothing in this world to be afraid of. Or to put it simply: "My Dad can beat up your dad."

If someone is struggling with addiction, struggling with paying rent, struggling with anger, struggling with fear, anxieties, worries, or depression—this one truth can set them free from it all. My Dad can beat up your dad. God is stronger than anything anyone will ever face. And God loves unconditionally. He will always love with an everlasting love, as He told Jeremiah.

So whatever fear might come in, when believers better understand the love of God and better come to know it— *ginōskō*, experientially—they can then better believe in it regarding the things they cannot see. All of a sudden fears can go away, worries can go away, and there is now power and strength to face whatever circumstances arise.

Fear Involves Punishment

The verse goes on to say, "Because fear involves torment." A better translation, and most other Bible versions render it this way, is "fear involves punishment." It is an uncommon word in the Bible, appearing only twice, and in the other instance it is translated as punishment.

As a Christian, one never has to fear being punished by God. A lot of people feel that way—"I feel like God is punishing me." But it is important to understand the difference between punishment and chastisement, because this is the difference between scary fear and reverential fear of a father who loves.

When thinking about fear of punishment, the character Grand Moff Tarkin from Star Wars comes to mind: "Fear will keep the local systems in line. Fear of this battle station." The Death Star. Mess with the Empire, and they blow up your planet.

But consider: does blowing up a planet teach anyone any lessons? It doesn't teach anything because everyone is dead. The whole planet is gone. Punishment is not intended to teach. The death penalty exists as a punishment; there are consequences for actions. But it is not intended to teach anything to the one being punished. Perhaps fear will stop someone from doing something because they fear the punishment. But that is not how God works.

God chastises.

> *"My son, do not despise the chastening of*
> *the LORD, nor be discouraged when you are*
> *rebuked by Him; for whom the LORD loves*
> *He chastens, and scourges every son whom*
> *He receives."* (Hebrews 12:5–6)

"Chastening" is really just a fancy word for discipline or correction. In short, there is no fear in the love of God and in understanding God's love, because scary fear involves punishment and torment. But believers do not need to fear that at all.

If God is doing something that feels hard to go through, it is because a loving Father is trying to teach a lesson, or send a signal, or get His child back on track. Think of it this way: no one likes it if someone comes up from behind unexpectedly and grabs the back of their shirt and yanks hard. It chokes and throws them backward. But if they are walking off a cliff, they probably will not complain too much.

What believers need to realize is that God is never going to yank them, poke them, or lay a burden upon them to punish them—because every punishment they deserved was placed upon Jesus on the cross.

Human beings have this tendency to like beating themselves up. "I am so bad. I cannot believe I did these horrible things. I just need to kick the crap out of myself and maybe that will make me feel better." But this is actually almost insulting to God. Because if every sin was laid on Jesus Christ on the cross, then if someone is beating themselves up, it is kind of like saying, "Well, that was not good enough. I have to add something to it. That punishment was not great enough. I need to do more."

The reality is no. There is no punishment in the love of God. He may do things to correct. He may do things to get attention. He may put believers through something to make them stronger so they can face even greater things or minister to those in need. But a loving Father is not going to punish His kids.

This is something parents need to remember too. We are not called to punish our kids, but we are called to chastise them. And there is a difference. The heart is different. The intent is different. And quite often the means are different.

So when the text says, "There is no fear in love, but perfect love casts out fear, because fear involves torment. But he who fears has not been made perfect in love," the application is clear:

If believers understand the love of God—that "my Dad is bigger than your dad"—they have no reason to fear in this life.

> "...casting all your care upon Him, for He cares for you." (1 Peter 5:7)

178

God loves believers. He cares about them. They have no reason to fear anything, because an all-loving, all-powerful, and all-knowing God demonstrated His love for them in that while they were still sinners, Christ died for them. As 1 John 3:16 says, "By this we know love, because He laid down His life for us."

We Love Him Because He First Loved Us

"We love Him because He first loved us."
(1 John 4:19)

This brings us to the final verse in this passage. Charles Spurgeon wrote five sermons on this one little verse alone. There is such richness in it.

If believers dive into how much God loves them, it will fix a lot of problems they have been trying to fix other ways. It works backwards from what many expect. The feeling is often, "I need to do all this stuff." But it works differently.

Spurgeon wrote:

"Yet we must not try to make ourselves love our Lord, but look to Christ's love first, for His love to us will beget in us love to Him. I know that some of you are greatly distressed because you cannot love Christ as much as you would like to do, and you keep on fretting because it is so. Now, just forget your own love to Him and think of His great love to you. And then immediately your love will come to something more like that which you desire it to be."

Elsewhere Spurgeon said:

"Now remember, we never make ourselves love Christ more by flogging ourselves for not loving Him more. We come to love those better whom we love by knowing them

179

better. If you want to love Christ more, think more of Him. Think more of what you have received from Him."

Believers will love Him even more as they grow in the knowledge and belief that He loved them first. The deeper they go into that understanding, the greater their belief and faith will become. They need to trust Him, because the understanding comes first and then the belief comes second.

When Feelings Fail

C.S. Lewis said, "Though our feelings come and go, God's love for us does not."

Remember: believers change, but God does not change. If someone has ever felt loved by God—good. Nothing has changed. Nothing has changed at all.

Spurgeon said, "To feel God's love is very precious, but to believe it when you do not feel it is the noblest." He was making the point that it is not easy. It is not easy at all. Sometimes believers do not feel it, but they have to trust that God, who has done all these other things, will still love them and be faithful to them even when they cannot feel it.

Richard Sibbes wrote:

"Measure not God's love and favor by your own feeling. The sun shines as clearly in the darkest day as it does in the brightest. The difference is not in the sun, but in some clouds which hinder the manifestation of the light thereof."

The sun is always the same brightness. It does not change, and it is always there. Sometimes it is on the other side of the earth. Sometimes it is behind the clouds. But the point is that it does not change—just like the love of God does not change. Sometimes believers have a hard time seeing it, but it is still just the same. It is still right there.

The Cross: The Proof of God's Love

And if believers are struggling with remembering and believing the love of God, Billy Graham said, "God proved His love on the cross. When Christ hung and bled and died, it was God saying to the world, 'I love you.'"

There are two things Christians have seen and heard so much that they might treat them as commonplace: "Jesus loves you," and the cross. We wear it. We have seen it. We drive by it. But we must remember that the cross was there to show us God's love. He demonstrated His love for us on the cross.

It is not just a symbol of sin being forgiven. It is a symbol that says, "I love you, and this is how much I love you." Do you know it? Have you felt it?

F.B. Meyer said, "Calvary is the great proof of the love of God. When we doubt Him, we have only to think of the cross."

How insulted would someone be if they gave up their child for another person, and that person felt it was not good enough? "I don't know if that shows me that you really care." It is remembering that simple thing—that God gave His Son to show He really cares.

The Puritan Richard Baxter wrote, "O cross! It is Thy love that draws me, Thy love that holds me, Thy love that will not let me go."

We look to the cross and remember that this is God saying, "I love you this much."

181

Conclusion: Known and Believed

Returning to the very first words of verse 16: "We have known and believed the love that God has for us."

If someone has known the love of God—experiential knowledge, *ginōskō*—then they know that they know. There is no doubt. If someone has been shocked by household electricity, they know what it felt like. They did not wonder, "Was I shocked or not?" Once someone actually gets shocked, they know they were shocked. If someone has been burned by fire, they know fire is hot. No one can ever convince them otherwise.

And if the Holy Spirit has taken up residence in someone's heart—as He does with every single born-again person who becomes a Christian—they know it, because they have experientially felt and now know and understand the love of God. And it is that knowledge which carries them forward so they can believe all the things they need to believe.

If someone needs to grow in their faith and have help in believing, then they need to go back and continually be experiencing the love of God that He has for them.

The prayer is that all believers not only have experienced God's love, but continue to experience it and grow in the knowledge of God's love as He tries to complete and perfect that work He has begun—which He promises to finish:

> *"...being confident of this very thing, that He who has begun a good work in you will complete it until the day of Jesus Christ."*
> (Philippians 1:6)

Faith, Love, and Obedience
1 John 4:20–5:5

Introduction: The Inseparable Triad

As noted previously, the chapter divisions in First John
often fall at awkward points. Verses 20 and 21 of chapter
four belong thematically with the opening of chapter five,
forming a unified section that runs from 4:20 through 5:5.
In this passage, John weaves together three inseparable
realities: belief, love, and obedience. For John, these are
not three separate concerns but one integrated whole. If you
believe, you will love and you will obey. And if you love
and obey, it demonstrates that you truly believe.

The Test of Visible Love

> *If someone says, "I love God," and hates his*
> *brother, he is a liar; for he who does not*
> *love his brother whom he has seen, how can*
> *he love God whom he has not seen? And this*
> *commandment we have from Him: that he*
> *who loves God must love his brother also.*
> *(1 John 4:20–21)*

John's logic here is devastatingly simple. It is actually
easier to love someone you can see and interact with than
to love the invisible God. If a person cannot manage the
easier task—loving a visible brother—how can they claim
success at the harder one? The visible is the proving ground
for the invisible.

There is another angle to consider: it is easier to fake loving
a God you cannot see. Anyone can claim devotion to an
invisible deity. But claims of loving God are tested by

observable behavior toward people. As James would say, "Prove it. Prove it with your works." The demons believe in one God—they do well to believe—but their belief produces nothing but trembling, not obedience.

The Paralytic and the Proof

In Mark 2, when Jesus encountered the paralytic lowered through the roof, He first declared, "Son, your sins are forgiven you." The scribes objected: "Who can forgive sins but God alone?" They were right in one sense—anyone can claim to forgive sins, but how would you verify such a spiritual transaction? So Jesus provided visible proof: "Which is easier, to say to the paralytic, 'Your sins are forgiven you,' or to say, 'Arise, take up your bed and walk'?" Then He commanded the man to rise, and he did.

Jesus gave them a physical, tangible miracle so they could believe the spiritual reality. John applies the same principle here. Someone claims to love God—that is a spiritual assertion impossible to verify directly. But can that person demonstrate love for a brother right in front of them? That is testable. If they hate their brother, then their claim to love God is exposed as a lie. The truth is simply not in them.

The Command That Binds Them Together

Verse 21 makes explicit what was implicit: this is a commandment from God Himself. He who loves God must love his brother also. The word "must" carries the force of obligation. This is not optional. This is not merely recommended for the spiritually mature. If you love God, loving your brother is required.

Believing in the Right Jesus

> *Whoever believes that Jesus is the Christ is*
> *born of God, and everyone who loves Him*
> *who begot also loves him who is begotten of*
> *Him. (1 John 5:1)*

The phrase "Jesus is the Christ" carries significant weight in light of the heresy John was combating. Cerinthianism taught that the Christ spirit descended upon the *man* Jesus at His baptism and then departed before His crucifixion. According to this view, Jesus and the Christ were separable—one a mere man, the other a spirit that temporarily inhabited him.

John's confession demolishes this heresy. Jesus is the Christ—not a man who received the Christ spirit, but the Christ Himself. To believe this is to be born of God. This is essential Christian doctrine. You must believe in the right Jesus to be a genuine believer. As we examined previously, the Jesus of the Jehovah's Witnesses and the Jesus of the Mormons is not the Jesus of Scripture. Believing in a different Jesus—however sincere that belief may be—does not result in salvation.

Loving the Father Means Loving the Son

The second half of verse one establishes another non-negotiable connection: everyone who loves Him who begot (the Father) also loves him who is begotten of Him (the Son). You cannot claim to love God the Father while rejecting Jesus Christ. If you love the begetter, you will love the only begotten Son.

This has immediate application for those who wish to affirm monotheism while denying Christ. Many claim to worship the God of Abraham while rejecting Jesus as the

185

Messiah. But John insists this is impossible. To reject Jesus is to reject the Father. There is no way to the Father except through the Son.

Love Demonstrated Through Obedience

By this we know that we love the children of God, when we love God and keep His commandments. For this is the love of God, that we keep His commandments. And His commandments are not burdensome.
(1 John 5:2–3)

Verse two might seem to reverse what John has been saying. Throughout this letter, he has argued that loving the brethren demonstrates our love for God. Now he says we know we love the children of God when we love God and keep His commandments. The logic runs both directions because the realities are inseparable.

The practical application is significant: truly loving our brethren means we will love God and keep His commandments, and we will encourage, empower, and help our brothers and sisters do the same. When we see fellow believers caught in sin, genuine love does not remain silent. Genuine love speaks the truth. If we really love our brethren, we will want them to love God and keep His commandments—and we will do what we can to help them toward that end.

This Is the Love of God

Verse three provides one of John's clearest statements on the relationship between love and obedience: "This is the love of God, that we keep His commandments." The connection is open and shut, clear as day. When people claim to love God while living in habitual sin, there is a glaring problem. John has made this point five or six times throughout this epistle, stating the same truth in slightly different arrangements of words. The repetition is intentional.

Why does John keep saying the same thing? Because we keep failing to live it. If a wife keeps repeating something to her husband, there is probably a reason—he is not doing what needs to be done. John keeps reminding us because we are not obeying as we ought. Each repetition is meant to sink a little deeper, penetrate our callous hearts, and remind us of the high calling God has placed on our lives.

The hard truth must be stated plainly: you cannot love God and not be a Christian. That does not work. You cannot love God and hate the church. You cannot love God and despise His Word. You cannot love God and love sin simultaneously. These things are mutually exclusive. You cannot really love your wife while maintaining a mistress. There is a fundamental disconnect. "Well, I really do love her, but..." No. John is hammering this home.

His Commandments Are Not Burdensome

The final phrase of verse three offers remarkable encouragement: "His commandments are not burdensome." The Greek word describes a heavy weight that must be borne. John insists that God's commands are not that kind of crushing load.

Why not? Because love lightens any burden. When we truly love God, His commandments do not feel oppressive. Consider how young people act when they fall in love. A teenage boy who had to be forced to brush his teeth and wear deodorant suddenly starts checking himself in the mirror and sniffing his shirt before walking out the door—

because he has fallen in love. Things that were once burdensome become effortless when love is the motivation.

Romans 12:1 captures this principle: *"I beseech you therefore, brethren, by the mercies of God, that you present your bodies a living sacrifice, holy, acceptable to God, which is your reasonable service."* Presenting our whole bodies as living sacrifices sounds burdensome—until we read that it is our "reasonable service." When we are in love with God, it seems and feels reasonable.

Loving God is keeping His commandments. It is not about following rules so that God will love us. Rather, knowing that a loving God has given us commands to protect us, uplift us, and mature us, we trust Him enough to obey. When I love Him and trust Him, obeying simply makes sense.

Overcoming by Faith

For whatever is born of God overcomes the world. And this is the victory that has overcome the world—our faith. Who is he who overcomes the world, but he who believes that Jesus is the Son of God? (1 John 5:4–5)

These verses shift the emphasis to overcoming. When we are born of God, we overcome the world. And the instrument of that victory is faith—specifically, faith in Jesus as the Son of God.

The language of overcoming resonates throughout Scripture and reaches its fullest expression in the book of Revelation. In chapters two and three, Jesus addresses seven churches, and to each one He extends a promise to "him who overcomes." These promises are worth noting as they illuminate what John means by overcoming.

The Promises to Overcomers

To Ephesus, Christ promises: "To him who overcomes I will give to eat from the tree of life, which is in the midst of the Paradise of God." To Smyrna, the persecuted church whose members had already faced martyrdom: "He who overcomes shall not be hurt by the second death." To Pergamos: "To him who overcomes I will give some of the hidden manna to eat. And I will give him a white stone, and on the stone a new name written which no one knows except him who receives it."

To Thyatira: "He who overcomes, and keeps My works until the end, to him I will give power over the nations." To Sardis: "He who overcomes shall be clothed in white garments, and I will not blot out his name from the Book of Life; but I will confess his name before My Father and before His angels." To Philadelphia: "He who overcomes, I will make him a pillar in the temple of My God, and he shall go out no more. I will write on him the name of My God and the name of the city of My God, the New Jerusalem, which comes down out of heaven from My God. And I will write on him My new name."

And to Laodicea: "To him who overcomes I will grant to sit with Me on My throne, as I also overcame and sat down with My Father on His throne."

Faith Is the Victory

Every believer will face trials, temptations, and opposition. The world presses in from every side. What do we need to overcome whatever comes against us? Faith. "This is the victory that has overcome the world—our faith."

Revelation 12:11 describes how the tribulation saints will overcome: *"They overcame him by the blood of the Lamb and by the word of their testimony, and they did not love their lives to the death."* Faith in the blood of the Lamb and faithful testimony to Christ—that is how overcoming happens.

This should encourage every believer. You are never ill-equipped for what you face. God will only allow you to encounter that which you need your faith to conquer. The resources are sufficient. The victory is assured for those who believe.

The Essential Confession

Verse five returns to the christological confession: "Who is he who overcomes the world, but he who believes that Jesus is the Son of God?" Again John emphasizes believing in the right Jesus—not a created being, not a spirit-anointed man, but the eternal Son of God who took on human flesh.

This is where John has been driving throughout this section. Faith, love, and obedience are not three separate tracks but one integrated reality. Genuine faith in Jesus as the Son of God produces love for God and love for the brethren. That love expresses itself in obedience to God's commands. And that obedient faith overcomes the world.

Excursus: Signs That God Is in a Church

Before leaving this section, it is worth addressing a question that naturally arises from John's teaching: How do we know God is present in a church? Various answers have been proposed, and not all of them align with what John emphasizes.

Power, Signs, and Wonders?

Some would say that signs and miracles prove God's presence. If people see demonstrations of supernatural power, they will know this is a real church. But we should remember 2 Thessalonians 2:9: "The coming of the lawless one is according to the working of Satan, with all power, signs, and lying wonders." Yes, we should expect God to work miraculously among His people. But miraculous activity is not the definitive sign of God's approval, because the Antichrist will come doing miraculous things through the false prophet.

Popularity?

Others suggest that attendance proves authenticity. If multitudes flock to a church, surely God must be blessing it. But Jesus warned: "Enter by the narrow gate; for wide is the gate and broad is the way that leads to destruction, and there are many who go in by it. Because narrow is the gate and difficult is the way which leads to life, and there are few who find it." Popularity is not a reliable indicator. Some churches draw large crowds precisely because they preach a gospel that does not offend, that never rubs anyone the wrong way.

The ministry of the Word should challenge us. A pastor's role includes elements of a trainer—if people can come and go without ever feeling the weight of conviction, without ever being pushed to grow, no real development is occurring. The goal is not to injure, but neither is it to leave people comfortable in their complacency.

Emotion and Passion?

Still others point to emotional intensity as proof of God's presence. If people feel deeply moved, if there is great passion in the worship, surely God is at work. And yes, we want passion. We want genuine emotion paired with truth and the experience of God. But emotion alone can be manufactured. Surface-level feelings can be stirred without deep roots being established.

Jesus addressed this in the parable of the sower. The seed that fell on stony ground was received immediately with joy—but it had no root, and when tribulation came, that person stumbled. Outward emotional response does not guarantee inward spiritual reality.

Love: The True Mark

So what does identify a genuine work of God? John's answer throughout this letter is unmistakable: love. Sacrificial love. The kind of love that costs something. The kind of love that is not easy or fun but pours itself out for others regardless.

Where there is no love, there is no genuine Christianity— no matter how many miracles, how large the crowds, or how intense the emotions. And this love must be paired with truth. There is no love in lying to people. When we see brothers and sisters in sin and remain silent, that is not love; it is cruelty. Biblical love does what it takes to help people, sacrificing again and again to bring them to maturity in Christ.

Conclusion

This brief passage packs enormous theological weight into a few verses. John binds together faith, love, and obedience as an inseparable triad. Genuine faith in Jesus as the Christ and the Son of God produces genuine love for God and for fellow believers. That love demonstrates itself through obedience to God's commands—commands that are not burdensome when we truly love Him. And that believing, loving, obedient life overcomes the world.

The tests John provides are uncomfortable but necessary. Do we love our brothers and sisters in tangible, observable ways? Do we keep God's commandments not as a crushing burden but as a reasonable expression of our love? Do we believe in the Jesus of Scripture—the eternal Son who came in the flesh—or some other Jesus of human invention?

The promises to overcomers in Revelation await those who persevere in this faith. The tree of life, protection from the second death, hidden manna, white stones with new names, authority over nations, white garments, permanent places in God's temple, seats on Christ's throne—these await those who overcome by faith. And that faith is simply this: believing that Jesus is the Son of God and living accordingly.

The Epistles of John

The Witness of God
1 John 5:6–13

The Testimony of Water and Blood

> *This is He who came by water and blood—*
> *Jesus Christ; not only by water, but by water*
> *and blood. And it is the Spirit who bears*
> *witness, because the Spirit is truth.*
> *(1 John 5:6)*

This verse has been interpreted in various ways throughout church history. Some, including Calvin and Luther, understood the water and blood as symbolic references to baptism and communion. The connection is understandable—water relates to baptism, blood to the Lord's Supper. However, this interpretation does not adequately explain how these would serve as testimony that Jesus "came," which is John's point.

Augustine suggested the water and blood refer to what flowed from Christ's side when the soldier pierced Him on the cross. Many readers, encountering "blood and water" paired together, immediately recall that scene from John 19. Yet again, it is difficult to see how that event alone would testify to who Jesus is in the way John describes.

The Best Interpretation: Baptism and Crucifixion

Tertullian, an early church father predating Calvin, Luther, and Augustine on this matter, believed the water and blood refer to Jesus's baptism and crucifixion respectively. This interpretation has gained the support of the majority of modern scholarship, and once the connections are understood, it becomes the most compelling view.

Remember Cerinthus? According to his reasoning God would not allow the Christ spirit to die on the cross. In this heresy, Jesus was merely a man temporarily indwelt by a divine spirit.

Many scholars believe that "water and blood" may have been terminology Cerinthus himself used. John's readers would have recognized these words as referring to baptism (water) and crucifixion (blood). Cerinthus acknowledged the water—the Christ spirit came at baptism—but denied that the Christ was present at the blood, the crucifixion.

John's emphatic response is: "not only by water, but by water and blood." Jesus was testified to at both events. At His baptism, the heavens opened, the Father spoke from heaven declaring "This is My beloved Son, in whom I am well pleased," and the Holy Spirit descended in the form of a dove. There was unmistakable testimony that Jesus was the Son of God.

But there was also testimony at the crucifixion. The Gospel of John records that just before the crucifixion, God spoke again from heaven. At the cross itself, the sun darkened, earthquakes shook the land, graves opened and the dead walked, and the veil of the temple was torn from top to bottom. And three days later, Jesus rose from the dead. The water and the blood both testify: Jesus is the Christ, the Son of God, from the beginning of His ministry to its climax— and He remains so forever.

Excursus: The Johannine Comma

For readers who are less interested in manuscript transmission, this section may be skimmed or skipped without affecting the overall argument of the passage.

> *For there are three that bear witness in heaven: the Father, the Word, and the Holy Spirit; and these three are one. And there are three that bear witness on earth: the Spirit, the water, and the blood; and these three agree as one. (1 John 5:7–8, NKJV)*

What we have just read is known as the Johannine Comma—"Johannine" being another form of "John" (from Latin and Greek), and "comma" referring to a clause or short passage. This is the most controversial piece of Scripture in the entire Bible, with ongoing debate about whether it belongs in the text at all.

The majority of scholars, including many conservative ones, argue that this passage should be removed. To illustrate the difference, here is how the NASB renders these verses, omitting the disputed portion:

> *For there are three that testify: the Spirit and the water and the blood; and the three are in agreement. (1 John 5:7–8, NASB)*

Everything between "in heaven" and "on earth"—the Father, the Word, the Holy Spirit, and "these three are one"—is absent from this translation. Why such a dramatic difference?

The Argument Against the Comma

The common argument runs as follows: There are over 5,000 Greek manuscripts of the New Testament, and only

197

about ten later manuscripts contain the Johannine Comma. The evidence seems overwhelming at first glance.

However, this presentation is somewhat misleading. Of those 5,000 manuscripts, only about 500 actually contain First John—most manuscripts do not include every New Testament book. And of those 500, only about a dozen contain these particular verses at all, with or without the comma. So the pool of relevant manuscripts is much smaller than initially suggested.

Furthermore, when Jerome translated the Bible into Latin around AD 405, Latin became the dominant language of Scripture in the Western church. Greek manuscript production largely ceased except in Greek-speaking churches. So we must look beyond Greek manuscripts to assess this question.

The Greek manuscripts that lack the comma include the famous codices: Codex Sinaiticus (mid-300s), Codex Vaticanus (mid-300s), and Codex Alexandrinus (early 400s). The Greek manuscripts that include the comma are significantly later—10th century and beyond—and in some cases the words appear only in the margin rather than the main text.

The Argument For the Comma

Despite the manuscript evidence, several factors argue for the authenticity of the comma.

First, Jerome himself addressed this controversy in AD 405. When he completed the Vulgate, he wrote: *"In the first letter of John... much error has occurred at the hand of unfaithful translators contrary to the truth of faith, who have kept just the three words water, blood, and spirit in this edition, omitting the mention of the Father, Word, and*

Spirit." Jerome was aware that scribes were removing these words and considered it a corruption of the text.

Second, Socrates of Constantinople, writing church history around AD 439, noted a similar problem with 1 John 4:3. He observed: *"The removal of this passage out of ancient copies [was done] by those who wish to sever the divinity from the humanity... Some have corrupted this epistle, aiming at severing the humanity from the divinity."* There was a documented pattern of scribes altering texts to diminish the deity of Christ.

The Arian Connection

Understanding the historical context is crucial. Arius lived from approximately AD 256 to 336. He denied the deity of Christ, teaching that Jesus was a created being rather than eternal God. His influence grew so substantial that it prompted the Council of Nicaea in AD 325, where he was condemned as a heretic—and famously punched by St. Nicholas.

After Nicaea, Arius fled to Palestine and Egypt, regions where Roman authority was weaker. There he continued influencing church leaders. The Arian heresy gained so much traction in North Africa that Athanasius—the great defender of Trinitarian orthodoxy whose creed remains the finest statement on the Trinity—was actually exiled from Alexandria because the Arian faction had grown so powerful.

Here is the critical connection: Codex Vaticanus and Codex Sinaiticus were written during this exact period of Arian influence (mid-300s). Codex Alexandrinus came from Alexandria itself in the early 400s—the very region where Arianism was strongest. These manuscripts were produced during an era when there was documented motivation to remove texts affirming Christ's deity and the Trinity.

Early Church Fathers Knew the Comma

Third, church fathers before and during this period quoted the comma. Cyprian (AD 200–258) wrote: *"The Lord says, 'I and the Father are one.' And again it is written of the Father and of the Son and the Holy Spirit, 'and these three are one.'"* The phrase "these three are one" appears nowhere else in Scripture except the Johannine Comma. Cyprian clearly had access to this text.

Athanasius himself affirmed: *"In addition to all these, John affirms, 'and these three are one.'"* He attributed this statement to John's epistle.

Around AD 380, Priscillian of Avila wrote: *"As John says, there are three that give testimony on earth: the water, the flesh, and the blood, and these three are one. And there are three that give testimony in heaven: the Father and the Word and the Spirit, and these three are one in Christ Jesus."*

The Council of Carthage

Perhaps the most compelling evidence comes from the Council of Carthage in AD 484. Like the Council of Nicaea, this was a major gathering—350 bishops assembled to debate the nature of the Trinity and the deity of Christ. The attendees held varying positions; this was not a one-sided assembly.

At this council, Eugenius, speaking on behalf of Carthage, declared: *"And in order that we may teach until now more clearly than light that the Holy Spirit is now one divinity with the Father and the Son, it is proved by the evangelist*

John, for he says, 'There are three which bear testimony in heaven: the Father, the Word, and the Holy Spirit, and these three are one.'"

Why is this significant? Because 350 bishops were present, including those sympathetic to Arianism. If the Johannine Comma were not in their Scriptures, surely someone would have challenged Eugenius's appeal to it. The council proceedings are recorded, and no such challenge appears. The passage was apparently accepted as authentic Scripture by both sides of the debate.

The Grammar Argument

A fourth argument involves Greek grammar. In Greek, as in Spanish and other languages, nouns have grammatical gender. The word "three" must agree in gender with the nouns it modifies.

In the disputed passage, "Father" and "Word" are masculine nouns, while "Spirit," "water," and "blood" are neuter. When you have a mixture, Greek (like Spanish) defaults to the masculine form.

In the NASB rendering without the comma—"there are three that testify: the Spirit and the water and the blood"— the word "three" appears in masculine form, but all three nouns following it are neuter. This creates a grammatical irregularity.

With the comma included, the masculine nouns "Father" and "Word" justify the masculine form of "three," and the grammar works properly. One church father around AD 530 specifically made this argument, noting that removing the comma creates a grammatical problem that including it resolves.

201

The Umlaut in Vaticanus

Finally, even Codex Vaticanus—the oldest Greek manuscript containing these verses without the comma—has small dots (called an umlaut) in the margin next to this passage. Scribes used umlauts to mark places where they knew of textual variants. So even the scribe of Vaticanus was aware that other manuscripts contained different readings here. The controversy existed from the earliest texts we possess.

Summary and Conclusion

To summarize: The comma is missing from our oldest Greek manuscripts, but we have church fathers quoting it before those manuscripts were written. We have testimony from Jerome and others that scribes were deliberately removing these words. The manuscripts lacking the comma were produced during a period of intense Arian influence, when there was motive to eliminate Trinitarian proof texts. The grammar is problematic without the comma. And even the oldest manuscript lacking these words has a marginal note indicating awareness of the variant.

It is much easier to accidentally omit text while copying than to add it. A scribe whose eye skipped a line would not notice the omission, but inserted text would be immediately obvious to anyone familiar with the passage.

For these reasons, I believe the Johannine Comma belongs in our Bibles. This runs counter to many pastors and scholars I respect, who would remove it. But the historical evidence, in my judgment, supports its authenticity.

This is also why I favor the New King James Version, which is based on the Textus Receptus and Majority Text tradition rather than the Alexandrian texts (Vaticanus,

Sinaiticus, Alexandrinus) that underlie most modern translations. The differences extend beyond the Johannine Comma to numerous other passages—verses like Matthew 17:21, 18:11, 23:14, Mark 7:16, 9:44, 9:46, and many more are absent from many modern translations, along with the extended ending of Mark and the account of the woman caught in adultery in John 8.

You do not need the Johannine Comma to prove the Trinity—the doctrine is established throughout Scripture. But if it belongs in the Bible, then we have here a magnificent statement: "There are three that bear witness in heaven: the Father, the Word, and the Holy Spirit; and these three are one." This is the God we worship. To deny this is to believe in a different god entirely.

God's Witness Is Greater

> *If we receive the witness of men, the witness of God is greater; for this is the witness of God which He has testified of His Son. He who believes in the Son of God has the witness in himself; he who does not believe God has made Him a liar, because he has not believed the testimony that God has given of His Son. (1 John 5:9–10)*

John's argument is straightforward: We routinely accept human testimony. We believe the weatherman and pack accordingly for a camping trip. We trust doctors, lawyers, and teachers based on their word. If we readily accept the witness of fallible human beings, how much more should we accept the witness of God?

Notice also how verse nine connects to the full reading of verses seven and eight. The witnesses in heaven are the witness of God; the witnesses on earth are the witness of

203

men. The structure assumes both sets of witnesses mentioned in the preceding verses.

Verse ten introduces a sobering reality: he who believes in the Son of God has the witness in himself—the Holy Spirit, who dwells within every believer. But he who does not believe God has made Him a liar. To reject God's testimony about His Son is to call God a liar. There is no neutral ground here.

Eternal Life in the Son

And this is the testimony: that God has given us eternal life, and this life is in His Son. He who has the Son has life; he who does not have the Son of God does not have life. (1 John 5:11–12)

Here is God's testimony distilled to its essence: He has given us eternal life, and this life is found in His Son. The gift is not merely forgiveness, not merely heaven someday, but eternal life—life that begins the moment we believe and continues forever.

Verse twelve draws an absolute line: "He who has the Son has life; he who does not have the Son of God does not have life." John leaves no room for alternative paths to God. You cannot have the Father while rejecting the Son. You cannot claim to worship the God of Abraham while denying Jesus Christ.

This has immediate implications for interfaith dialogue. Do Muslims worship the same God? Not really—not if they reject the Son. Do Jewish people who reject Jesus as Messiah worship the same God? In a sense, perhaps, but they are denying the true nature of God when they deny the Son. There is no salvation apart from Jesus Christ. John has hammered this truth throughout his epistle, and here he states it with unmistakable clarity.

That You May Know

> *These things I have written to you who believe in the name of the Son of God, that you may know that you have eternal life, and that you may continue to believe in the name of the Son of God. (1 John 5:13)*

This verse reveals John's purpose in writing. He wrote his Gospel "that you may believe that Jesus is the Christ, the Son of God, and that believing you may have life in His name" (John 20:31). The Gospel was written to bring people to faith. The epistle was written so that those who already believe might have confidence and assurance of their salvation.

John has said challenging things throughout this letter. He has drawn sharp lines between genuine faith and false profession, between those who love and those who do not, between those who obey and those who live in sin. These tests could produce anxiety: "Am I really saved? Do I really love enough? Is my obedience sufficient?"

But John's purpose is not to create doubt—it is to establish assurance. He has written so that believers may know they have eternal life. The answer to the tests is simple: Do you love God? Do you believe in Jesus as the Son of God? Do you desire to obey His commands, even when you fail? Then you have nothing to fear. You possess eternal life.

Security and Assurance

As John MacArthur has noted, security is a fact, but assurance is a gift. The believer is secure whether they feel it or not—God does not revoke His gift of eternal life. But the experience of assurance, the confidence that we are truly His, is something God gives through His Word and Spirit.

Satan sows seeds of doubt. Believers wonder, get scared, question whether they truly belong to Christ. John wrote precisely to counter this: "I have written... that you may know." The Christian should not live in constant anxiety about salvation. The tests John provides are not designed to torment the sensitive conscience but to expose false profession and reassure genuine faith.

There is a theological tension here that different traditions resolve differently. Some emphasize God's sovereign election—if you are chosen, you can never be lost. But this can create anxiety: "How do I know if I'm chosen? Only if I endure to the end." Others emphasize human free will— you can freely accept salvation. But this too can create anxiety: "What if I mess it up? What if I lose what I've received?"

The biblical balance affirms both God's initiative and human response without the anxious implications of either extreme. God freely offers eternal life. We freely receive it. And once we are born again—once we have passed from death to life—we are His forever. He adopts us as children, and He does not un-adopt His children. We are born again, and He does not make us dead again.

Eternal life is spoken of throughout the New Testament as a present possession, not merely a future hope. We are "currently in possession of life eternal." It started when we were born again, when we passed from spiritual death to spiritual life, and it continues forever. The believer can know this and rest in it.

Conclusion

This passage centers on testimony and assurance. God has provided multiple witnesses to the truth about His Son—the testimony of the water at His baptism, the testimony of the blood at His crucifixion, the testimony of the Spirit who bears witness to truth. If we accept the Johannine Comma, we add the heavenly witnesses: the Father, the Word, and the Holy Spirit, who are one.

God's witness is greater than any human testimony we routinely accept. To reject this witness is to call God a liar. But to receive it is to possess eternal life—life that is found only in the Son. There is no alternative path, no other name, no way to the Father except through Jesus Christ.

And for those who believe, John offers this magnificent assurance: you may know that you have eternal life. Not hope, not wish, not wonder—know. This is the confidence available to every believer who trusts in the Son of God.

The Epistles of John

Confidence and Caution
1 John 5:14–21

Confidence in Prayer

> *Now this is the confidence that we have in*
> *Him, that if we ask anything according to*
> *His will, He hears us. And if we know that*
> *He hears us, whatever we ask, we know that*
> *we have the petitions that we have asked of*
> *Him. (1 John 5:14–15)*

Having established the believer's assurance of eternal life in verse 13, John now turns to a related confidence: assurance in prayer. The believer who knows he has eternal life can also know that God hears his prayers.

The key phrase is "according to His will." This is not a limitation designed to frustrate prayer but a liberation that brings peace. Psalm 37:4 promises that God will give us the desires of our heart—but that promise is given to those who delight in the Lord, whose hearts are aligned with His heart. When our desires match His will, we can pray with confidence.

Consider how Jesus Himself prayed in Gethsemane: "Father, if it is Your will, take this cup away from Me; nevertheless not My will, but Yours, be done." Jesus, fully man, facing a real death, asked if there was any other way—and then submitted to the Father's will. When we pray this way, God's will is always accomplished. If He answers our specific request, His will was done. If He does not answer as we asked, we can rest assured His will was still done.

Sometimes prayer is more for us than for God. God knows what will happen. But when we bring matters to Him in prayer, we are positioned to look back with confidence, knowing we took it to the Lord and trusted Him with the outcome. We may not always understand His will, but we can have confidence that when we pray, God hears, and His perfect will is being worked out.

Sin Leading to Death

> *If anyone sees his brother sinning a sin*
> *which does not lead to death, he will ask,*
> *and He will give him life for those who*
> *commit sin not leading to death. There is sin*
> *leading to death. I do not say that he should*
> *pray about that. All unrighteousness is sin,*
> *and there is sin not leading to death.*
> *(1 John 5:16–17)*

These two verses are among the most debated in the entire New Testament. There is perhaps no passage where commentators have offered such a diverse range of interpretations. When I first encountered these verses as a new believer, they confused me, and years of study have only confirmed that great minds see them very differently. Nevertheless, the text demands our attention, for it addresses how we should respond when we see fellow believers caught in sin.

What Is Sin?

John begins with a fundamental definition: "All unrighteousness is sin." The English word "sin" derives from an old archery term—you either hit the bullseye or you sinned. If God's holy perfection is the bullseye, then anytime we fall short of that standard, it is sin. This is humbling. Either we still sin, or we are as perfect as God. Since no one claims the latter, we must acknowledge the former. As John wrote earlier: "If we say that we have no sin, we deceive ourselves, and the truth is not in us" (1 John 1:8).

The Interpretive Challenge

The central question is: what is "sin leading to death"? Various interpretations have been proposed throughout church history. Some, reading the King James rendering "a sin unto death," have understood this as referring to the unpardonable sin—the blasphemy against the Holy Spirit. This interpretation flows from the indefinite article ("a sin") suggesting one specific sin.

However, the Greek language has no indefinite article. Greek has a definite article ("the") but uses no article where English would use "a" or "an." The translation could equally read "there is sin leading to death"—not one specific sin, but a category of sin.

Other proposed interpretations include: sins punishable by death under Mosaic law; sins that bring God's immediate physical judgment (as with Ananias and Sapphira in Acts 5, or those who abused communion in 1 Corinthians 11); sins carrying civil death penalties; or sins committed before versus after baptism. Each view has its advocates.

The Greek Grammar

The phrase "sin leading to death" in Greek is *hamartia pros thanaton*. The preposition pros means "toward" or "in the direction of." William Barclay noted that this describes "the sin which is going toward death, the sin whose boat is pointed in the direction of death, the sin which if continued must finish in death."

This suggests not a single act but a trajectory—sins that characterize a life heading toward destruction, not heaven. These are the kinds of sins John has already been talking about. Ones we would never expect a genuine believer to continue living in unrepentantly.

Biblical Lists of Disqualifying Sins

Paul provides such lists in his letters. To the Corinthians he wrote: *"Do you not know that the unrighteous will not inherit the kingdom of God? Do not be deceived. Neither fornicators, nor idolaters, nor adulterers, nor homosexuals, nor sodomites, nor thieves, nor covetous, nor drunkards, nor revilers, nor extortioners will inherit the kingdom of God"* (1 Corinthians 6:9–10). He immediately adds: "And such were some of you"—acknowledging that believers may have backgrounds in these sins. But the key word is "were." These are not lifestyles we expect Christians to continue living in.

Revelation offers a similar list: *"But the cowardly, unbelieving, abominable, murderers, sexually immoral, sorcerers, idolaters, and all liars shall have their part in the lake which burns with fire and brimstone"* (Revelation 21:8). People who persist in such things are heading toward death, not life.

Who Is the "Brother"?

John Stott made an astute observation: the text does not actually call the one committing sin unto death a "brother." It is the one whose sin does not lead to death who is termed a brother. The one whose sin leads to death is "neither named nor described." This may suggest that when someone persistently lives in sin leading to death, their status as a genuine brother becomes uncertain.

The distinction matters practically. If I encounter a fellow believer who is grumpy or says something unkind, I do not immediately question their salvation. Christians stumble. We get irritated. We have bad days. For such sins, John says to pray, and God will give that person life—not eternal life (which they already have) but the fullness of life, the vitality and blessing that sin disrupts.

But when someone claiming to be a Christian lives in willful, unrepentant rebellion—shacking up with a partner, getting drunk regularly, embracing lifestyles the Bible explicitly condemns—the situation is different. At that point, I genuinely do not know where they stand spiritually. Their actions cause me to fear for their soul.

When NOT to Just Pray

John's statement—"I do not say that he should pray about that"—does not mean we stop praying for people in serious sin. Jesus commanded us to pray even for our enemies. We never stop praying.

Rather, John is saying that prayer alone is not enough. There are times when we must do more than pray—we must speak, we must act. To see a professing believer heading toward destruction and merely pray from a distance would be unloving. Love requires intervention.

Paul addressed exactly this situation in 1 Corinthians 5, dealing with a man involved in sexual immorality with his stepmother. When the man refused correction, Paul instructed: *"I have written to you not to keep company with anyone named a brother, who is sexually immoral, or*

213

covetous, or an idolater, or a reviler, or a drunkard, or an extortioner—not even to eat with such a person" (1 Corinthians 5:11).

In that culture, eating with someone signified acceptance and intimate fellowship. Paul was not forbidding all contact but directing the church to withdraw the fellowship that implies approval. The goal, as Paul explains in verse 5, is "that his spirit may be saved in the day of the Lord Jesus." Even this severe action aims at restoration.

This is the course of action John implies: when sin leads toward death, do not merely pray—take action. Confront. Speak truth. If necessary, follow the church discipline process Jesus outlined in Matthew 18. Love requires it.

Three Things We Know

John concludes his letter with three affirmations, each beginning with "we know." These provide final assurance to believers.

We Know: The Born of God Does Not Continue in Sin

> *We know that whoever is born of God does not sin; but he who has been born of God keeps himself, and the wicked one does not touch him. (1 John 5:18)*

The phrase "does not sin" uses the Greek present tense, indicating continuous action. A better translation would be "does not continue in sin" or "does not make a practice of sin." This is consistent with everything John has said throughout his letter. Believers still sin, but they do not live in unrepentant sin. When they fall, they confess and are cleansed.

Some manuscripts read "God keeps him" rather than "keeps himself." Both readings are theologically true—Jude speaks of God being "able to keep you from stumbling" (Jude 24), while our present verse will soon command believers to "keep yourselves from idols." The believer's security involves both God's keeping power and human responsibility to guard against sin.

The Wicked One Does Not Touch Him

The word "touch" (Greek: haptomai) often means more than casual contact—it can mean "to cling to" or "to fasten onto." When Jesus told Mary Magdalene "Do not cling to Me," He used this word. When the woman with the issue of blood determined "If only I may touch His garment," she intended to grasp it firmly.

John's point is that Satan cannot cling to or take possession of the believer. This relates to the ongoing debate about whether Christians can be demon-possessed. Pastor Chuck Smith addressed this directly: "This business of the believer being possessed by demons and the supposed necessity of their deliverance... flies in the face of Scripture. 'The wicked one toucheth him not.'"

Several texts establish the believer's security: *"He who is in you is greater than he who is in the world"* (1 John 4:4). *"Submit to God. Resist the devil and he will flee from you"* (James 4:7). The shield of faith enables us to *"quench all the fiery darts of the wicked one"* (Ephesians 6:16).

This does not mean Satan has no influence. Scripture records Satan asking to sift Peter like wheat, filling Ananias's heart to lie, sending a messenger to buffet Paul, and hindering Paul's travel plans. Believers can be tempted, deceived, oppressed, and hindered. But Satan cannot

215

possess or own a believer who is indwelt by the Holy Spirit.

The greatest weapon against demonic influence is not a dramatic "power encounter" but a "truth encounter." Most Christians struggling with spiritual oppression simply need to understand the authority and protection they have in Christ. Ignorance of our spiritual resources allows the enemy to take advantage. When believers know the truth, the truth sets them free.

We Know: We Are of God

We know that we are of God, and the whole world lies under the sway of the wicked one. (1 John 5:19)

This verse draws a sharp line between two kingdoms. Believers are "of God"—they belong to Him, are born of Him, are kept by Him. The rest of the world lies under Satan's influence.

This perspective should shape how we view unbelievers. They are under the sway of the wicked one. We should not expect them to embrace biblical morality. They need salvation, not merely moral reformation. A young woman I knew in college wisely observed about an unbelieving professor: "He's not a believer. I can't expect anything from him. He doesn't need to be corrected in his views—he needs to get saved. Everything else will follow."

Christians sometimes exhaust themselves trying to reform the behavior of unbelievers. But people under Satan's sway will naturally reflect his values. The solution is not behavior modification but spiritual transformation through the gospel.

We Know: The Son Has Come

> *And we know that the Son of God has come*
> *and has given us an understanding, that we*
> *may know Him who is true; and we are in*
> *Him who is true, in His Son Jesus Christ.*
> *This is the true God and eternal life.*
> *(1 John 5:20)*

The third "we know" celebrates the incarnation and its benefits. The Son of God has come. He has given us understanding so that we may know the true God. And we are now in Him—in the Father and in His Son Jesus Christ.

The final phrase is striking: "This is the true God and eternal life." The antecedent of "this" is debated—does it refer to the Father or to Jesus Christ? Grammatically, it most naturally refers to the nearest noun, which is "Jesus Christ." John is affirming what he has maintained throughout this letter: Jesus Christ is the true God. He is eternal life. This is no created being, no spirit-anointed man, but God Himself in human flesh.

Keep Yourselves from Idols

> *Little children, keep yourselves from idols.*
> *Amen. (1 John 5:21)*

John's abrupt closing might seem disconnected from what precedes it, but it is profoundly relevant. Having established that we know the true God and are in Him, John warns against anything that would compete with that relationship.

It would be easy to dismiss this command as irrelevant—after all, we do not bow before carved statues. But as one commentator observed, "The greatest danger to your relationship with Jesus Christ is idolatry." An idol is anything that displaces God from His rightful place in our hearts and priorities.

Drifting Toward Idols

The book of Hebrews warns about drifting from the faith. But we rarely drift into empty space. We drift toward things—other interests, other loves, other priorities that gradually consume our time, our attention, our devotion. These become our idols.

Consider the order of God-given priorities: our relationship with God comes first. Second is our relationship with our spouse, if married. Third is raising our children. Fourth is ministry—the purpose for which God created us. After these come career, hobbies, and other legitimate pursuits. Anything that disrupts this order functions as an idol. It may not be sinful in itself, but when it displaces what should come first, it has become an object of worship.

The Modern Challenge

We live in an age of unprecedented temptation to idolatry. Previous generations never saw such beautiful people to envy, such possessions to covet, such experiences to crave. The constant stream of images and advertisements bombards us with things to desire—things we might never have wanted if we had never known they existed.

A hundred years ago, people did not covet automobiles they had never seen. They did not lust after lifestyles displayed on screens. They were not constantly presented with alternatives to contentment. Today, the internet provides instant access to the riches of biblical scholarship—and equally instant access to every form of evil. Social media shows us endless recipes, endless products, endless lives that seem more exciting than our own.

This is why John's final command is so urgent: "Little children, keep yourselves from idols." Be vigilant. Recognize when things begin displacing God-given priorities. When your career crowds out your marriage, when hobbies eclipse ministry, when entertainment consumes time meant for God—these are idol problems.

The warning applies especially to marriage. Relationships struggle today in part because of idolatry. Spouses who genuinely love each other find that love crowded out by competing loves—careers, children's activities, entertainment, social media. We know the priorities that make for a healthy marriage, yet "little things" constantly interfere. These little things are idols.

Conclusion

First John ends as it began—with confidence and challenge. We can have confidence in prayer, knowing that God hears us when we pray according to His will. We can have confidence in our spiritual security, knowing that the wicked one cannot possess us. We can have confidence in our identity as children of God, distinct from a world under Satan's sway. We can have confidence in our knowledge of the true God revealed in Jesus Christ.

But with confidence comes responsibility. We must discern when fellow believers need prayer and when they need intervention. We must recognize the difference between ordinary stumbling and sin that leads toward death. We must keep ourselves—actively guard ourselves—from the idols that compete for our devotion.

The Epistles of John

John has taken us on a journey through profound theological truths and intensely practical applications. He has shown us the nature of God as light and love. He has exposed the tests of genuine faith: belief in the right Jesus, obedient love for God, and sacrificial love for one another. He has warned against false teachers and the spirit of antichrist. He has provided assurance to those who truly believe and challenge to those merely professing.

And now, with the simplest of commands, he sends us out: "Little children, keep yourselves from idols." May we who know the true God refuse to give His place to any lesser thing.

Amen.

The Saving Doctrine of Christ
2 John

Late in John's life, after decades of faithful ministry and having watched all the other apostles pass from this earth, the aged apostle took up his pen to write to the elect lady and her children. This brief epistle, penned around AD 95-100, carries an urgent warning that remains as vital today as it was in the first century: beware of false teachers who preach a false doctrine of a different Christ, which cannot save.

The backdrop of this letter is critical to understanding its force. John was likely the last living apostle, having outlived Peter, Paul, James, and all the rest. Tradition places him in Ephesus in his old age, where he served as pastor until Emperor Domitian exiled him to the island of Patmos. There, in his late eighties, Jesus appeared to him and gave him the Revelation. After his release, John returned to Ephesus and wrote his Gospel and three epistles, of which Second John may well have been the final book of Scripture to be penned.

By this time, false teachers had multiplied throughout the churches. Chief among them were the Gnostics, a heretical group that denied core doctrines of the faith. They taught that Jesus was only spirit and did not have a real physical body, because they believed the flesh was inherently evil and only spirit was good. Therefore, if Jesus walked on a beach, He would leave no footprints, for He was merely a phantom. They also denied that Jesus was the Son of God. John addresses these lies head-on, both in his Gospel and in his epistles, emphasizing again and again that the apostles beheld Jesus, touched Him, heard Him, and witnessed His physical resurrection.

Thunder-voice John, as he was known in his youth, had mellowed in his old age. The early church fathers record that when he was too weak to preach at length, they would bring him out before the congregation and he would simply say, "Little children, love one another." Yet his love did not make him soft on error. In this epistle, he strikes a perfect balance: he emphasizes both truth and love, showing that genuine love requires doctrinal clarity, and genuine truth must be expressed in love.

The Greeting: Truth and Love

> *"The Elder, To the elect lady and her children, whom I love in truth, and not only I, but also all those who have known the truth, because of the truth which abides in us and will be with us forever: Grace, mercy, and peace will be with you from God the Father and from the Lord Jesus Christ, the Son of the Father, in truth and love."*
> *(2 John 1-3)*

John identifies himself simply as "the Elder." At this stage of his life, he needed no other title. Everyone knew who he was. He was the last man standing from those who had walked with Jesus in the flesh. He had reclined on Jesus' chest at the Last Supper. He had stood at the foot of the cross and received Jesus' mother Mary into his own care. He had outrun Peter to the empty tomb. He had seen the risen Lord and witnessed the ascension. And he had lived longer than any of the others, faithfully shepherding the church at Ephesus through tumultuous times.

The identity of "the elect lady and her children" has been debated. Some believe John was writing to an actual woman and her family. Others, including many early church fathers, understand this as symbolic language referring to a local church and its members. The Greek word for "elect" is the same word used elsewhere for God's chosen people, and "children" often refers to believers. Whichever view is correct, the message clearly addresses a body of believers who needed this warning.

What is unmistakable is John's emphasis on truth. In just the first four verses, he mentions truth five times. He loves them "in truth." All who have known the truth also love them. The truth abides in believers and will be with them forever. This heavy emphasis on truth is no accident. John is preparing them for the core message of the letter: there is such a thing as true doctrine and false doctrine, and the difference matters eternally.

When John says "the truth which abides in us and will be with us forever," he is speaking of Jesus Christ Himself, who declared, "I am the way, the truth, and the life" (John 14:6). But he is also speaking of the Holy Spirit, whom Jesus promised would abide with believers forever (John 14:16). Jesus, who is the truth, sent the Holy Spirit, and that Spirit abides in every true believer. The truth is not merely a set of propositions we mentally assent to; the truth is a Person who dwells within us.

John's greeting includes a beautiful triad: "Grace, mercy, and peace will be with you from God the Father and from the Lord Jesus Christ." But notice what he adds: "the Son of the Father." This was not superfluous. The Gnostics denied that Jesus was the Son of God. So John, even in his greeting, quietly but firmly affirms the truth. Jesus is the Son of the Father. This is not negotiable. This is not a secondary issue. This is the heart of the gospel.

And then comes that phrase: "in truth and love." These two themes will dominate the rest of the letter. Truth without love is cold and harsh. Love without truth is soft and spineless. But truth and love together create a foundation for genuine Christian fellowship and faithful ministry.

The Commandment: Love One Another

> *"I rejoiced greatly that I have found some of your children walking in truth, as we received commandment from the Father. And now I plead with you, lady, not as though I wrote a new commandment to you, but that which we have had from the beginning: that we love one another. This is love, that we walk according to His commandments. This is the commandment, that as you have heard from the beginning, you should walk in it." (2 John 4-6)*

John rejoices when he hears that some of the believers are walking in truth. This phrase, "walking in truth," appears again in Third John, where he writes, "I have no greater joy than to hear that my children walk in truth" (3 John 4). For a pastor in his nineties, having poured out his life for the gospel, there is no sweeter sound than hearing that those he has taught are living out what they have learned. Not merely believing it in their heads, but walking it out in their lives.

This distinction is crucial. James reminds us that even demons believe in God, and they tremble (James 2:19). Intellectual assent to doctrine is not saving faith. True faith evidences itself in a transformed life. When John commends these believers for "walking in truth," he is praising them for living out their confession. Their faith is not merely theoretical; it is active, visible, and real.

Then John transitions to the commandment of love. He says he is not writing them a new commandment, but rather the one they have had from the beginning. This echoes what he wrote in First John:

> *"Brethren, I write no new commandment to you, but an old commandment which you have had from the beginning. The old commandment is the word which you heard from the beginning. Again, a new commandment I write to you, which thing is true in Him and in you, because the darkness is passing away, and the true light is already shining." (1 John 2:7-8)*

What does John mean when he says the commandment is both old and new? The command to love is as old as the Law itself. But Jesus gave it a new depth and a new standard. On the night He was betrayed, Jesus told His disciples:

> *"A new commandment I give to you, that you love one another; as I have loved you, that you also love one another." (John 13:34)*

The commandment to love others is not new, but Jesus redefined love. It is no longer merely the golden rule—do unto others as you would have them do unto you. Now it is: love others as I have loved you. That is, with sacrificial, self-giving, agape love. This is the kind of love that lays down its life for friends. This is the love that washes feet. This is the love that goes to a cross.

In verse six, John ties love directly to obedience: "This is love, that we walk according to His commandments." And then he adds, "This is the commandment, that as you have heard from the beginning, you should walk in it." The

The Epistles of John

connection between love and obedience runs throughout
John's writings. Consider these words from Jesus, recorded
in John's Gospel:

> *"If you love Me, keep My commandments."*
> *(John 14:15)*

> *"If anyone loves Me, he will keep My word...*
> *He who does not love Me does not keep My*
> *words." (John 14:23-24)*

> *"If you keep My commandments, you will*
> *abide in My love, just as I have kept My*
> *Father's commandments and abide in His*
> *love." (John 15:10)*

And in his first epistle, John wrote:

> *"By this we know that we love the children*
> *of God, when we love God and keep His*
> *commandments. For this is the love of God,*
> *that we keep His commandments. And His*
> *commandments are not burdensome."*
> *(1 John 5:2-3)*

That last phrase is critical: "His commandments are not
burdensome." Why not? Because when you truly love
someone, serving them is not a burden—it is a joy. If a
husband says to his wife, "Look, I'm going on this walk
with you because I have to, not because I want to," that is
not love. But when love is genuine, we delight to do what
pleases the one we love. We are not looking for ways to
avoid obedience; we are looking for ways to express our
devotion.

This does not mean obedience is always easy. There are
struggles. There are temptations. There are battles with sin.
But the heart attitude is different. A person who loves God
is not thinking, "What can I get away with?" Rather, they

are thinking, "How can I honor Him?" When we stumble, we are grieved, not indifferent. We repent, not rationalize. We seek to make it right, not to minimize it.

If someone claims to be a Christian but views God's commandments as burdensome restrictions, that is a red flag. It suggests the heart has not been regenerated. An unbeliever sees God's laws as oppressive. A true believer sees them as loving guidance from a good Father who knows what is best for His children. God calls certain things sin not to ruin our fun, but because those things harm us or harm others. Every commandment in Scripture is either for our protection or for the protection of others, because God loves us.

The Warning: Deceivers and Antichrists

"For many deceivers have gone out into the world who do not confess Jesus Christ as coming in the flesh. This is a deceiver and an antichrist." (2 John 7)

Now John shifts from love to the reason he is writing: false teachers are spreading false doctrine, and the church must be on guard. He calls these false teachers "deceivers" and "antichrists." Both terms are strong. A deceiver is one who deliberately misleads. An antichrist is one who opposes Christ or seeks to replace Him.

The specific heresy John addresses here is the denial that Jesus came in the flesh. The Gnostics taught that Jesus was purely spirit, not truly human. They could not accept that God would take on a physical body, because they viewed matter as evil and spirit as good. Therefore, they reasoned, Jesus must have only appeared to be human. This heresy is called Docetism, from the Greek word meaning "to seem" or "to appear."

227

But this teaching strikes at the heart of the gospel. If Jesus did not truly take on human flesh, then He did not truly die. If He did not truly die, there was no atonement. If there was no atonement, we are still in our sins. The incarnation is not a peripheral doctrine. It is central to our salvation.

John emphasizes this again and again in his writings. In his Gospel, he writes, "The Word became flesh and dwelt among us" (John 1:14). In his first epistle, he says:

> *"That which was from the beginning, which we have heard, which we have seen with our eyes, which we have looked upon, and our hands have handled, concerning the Word of life—the life was manifested, and we have seen, and bear witness, and declare to you that eternal life which was with the Father and was manifested to us—that which we have seen and heard we declare to you."*
> *(1 John 1:1-3)*

John is saying: I was there. I heard Him speak. I saw Him with my own eyes. I touched Him with my own hands. He was not a phantom. He was flesh and blood. He ate fish. He grew tired. He wept. He bled. And He rose again in a physical, glorified body. Anyone who denies this is teaching another gospel.

John also warns in First John:

> *"Beloved, do not believe every spirit, but test the spirits, whether they are of God; because many false prophets have gone out into the world." (1 John 4:1)*

Not every claim to speak for God is true. Not every passionate preacher is preaching truth. Not every miracle-worker is working miracles by God's power. We are commanded to test the spirits. How? By comparing what is taught with what Scripture teaches. If someone claims, "God told me," but what they say contradicts Scripture, then God did not tell them. God does not contradict Himself.

It is worth pausing here to address the modern tendency to claim direct revelation from God. Some people seem to have a direct hotline to heaven and are constantly saying, "God told me this" and "God told me that." While we believe God can and does speak to His people, we must be cautious. If God truly tells someone something, that is the ultimate trump card—there is no arguing with it. But precisely because it is so powerful, we must be careful not to misuse it.

The Apostle Paul gives us guidance for handling prophetic words in the church. In First Corinthians 14, he instructs that if someone shares a word from the Lord in a gathering of believers, others should weigh what was said. A humble approach might be, "I sense the Lord may be saying..." or "I believe the Lord is encouraging us to..." This allows room for testing and correction, whereas "Thus says the Lord!" shuts down all discussion and makes the speaker unanswerable.

John also addresses the origin of these false teachers in his first epistle:

> *"They went out from us, but they were not of us; for if they had been of us, they would have continued with us; but they went out that they might be made manifest, that none of them were of us." (1 John 2:19)*

Some false teachers come from outside the church, but others arise from within. They sit in the pews for years. They may even serve in ministry. But eventually, they depart from the truth and lead others astray. When they leave, it becomes clear they were never truly born again. They had a form of godliness but not the power. They had a confession but not a conversion.

This is a sobering reality. Over the years, many who once seemed strong in the faith have fallen away. Some have embraced theological error. Others have fallen into moral sin and never repented. Still others have simply walked away from the faith entirely. And in each case, we are left to wonder: Were they ever truly saved, or did they merely have an emotional experience that looked like salvation but was not?

The Exhortation: Guard Your Reward

"Look to yourselves, that we do not lose those things we worked for, but that we may receive a full reward." (2 John 8)

This verse has caused some debate among commentators. Is John warning believers that they might lose their salvation? No. The New Testament is clear that those who are truly born again are kept by the power of God (1 Peter 1:5). Jesus said, "I give them eternal life, and they shall never perish; neither shall anyone snatch them out of My hand" (John 10:28). Our security rests not on our grip on God, but on His grip on us.

So what does it mean to "lose those things we worked for" and to forfeit a "full reward"? John seems to be addressing two groups of people. First, there are false teachers who were never truly saved. They appeared to be part of the church, but they have now departed from the truth, revealing their unregenerate state. For them, there is no reward at all, only judgment.

Second, there are genuine believers who may be led astray by false teaching. Though they are saved by grace, they may lose rewards they would have otherwise received. The New Testament teaches that while salvation is by grace alone through faith alone, there will be rewards in heaven based on how we lived as believers. Paul writes:

> *"Each one's work will become clear; for the Day will declare it, because it will be revealed by fire; and the fire will test each one's work, of what sort it is. If anyone's work which he has built on it endures, he will receive a reward. If anyone's work is burned, he will suffer loss; but he himself will be saved, yet so as through fire." (1 Cor. 3:13-15)*

A believer who is deceived into following false teaching may waste years of their life. They may lead others astray. They may fail to grow in godliness. And though they are still saved, they will have little to show for their time on earth. They will enter heaven, but with nothing to lay at Jesus' feet. This is what John is warning against.

There is also a warning here for those who work hard in ministry. Pastors, teachers, evangelists, and faithful laypeople invest their lives in the gospel. They study, preach, teach, counsel, disciple, and serve. But if those they have poured into are later deceived and led away from the truth, some of that work is lost. The people may still be saved, but the fruit of years of labor is diminished.

This is why false teaching is so dangerous. It does not merely affect the false teacher. It affects everyone who listens to them. It steals truth from the minds of believers. It cripples the growth of the church. It robs God of glory. And it leads precious souls into confusion and error.

The Test: Abiding in the Doctrine of Christ

> *"Whoever transgresses and does not abide*
> *in the doctrine of Christ does not have God.*
> *He who abides in the doctrine of Christ has*
> *both the Father and the Son." (2 John 9)*

Here is the test: Do you abide in the doctrine of Christ? The word "transgresses" can also be translated "goes beyond" or "goes ahead." It refers to those who claim to have advanced beyond the basic teachings of the apostles. They offer "deeper truths" or "a better way" to know God. They suggest that the simple gospel is just Christianity 101, but they have something more profound to offer.

But John says plainly: if you do not abide in the doctrine of Christ, you do not have God. Period. There is no secret knowledge. There is no higher level of spirituality that goes beyond what the apostles taught. Christ is the way, the truth, and the life, and no one comes to the Father except through Him (John 14:6). If you have Christ, you have the Father. If you reject the true Christ, you have nothing.

This is where the gospel differs from every false religion and cult. Other systems add to Christ. They say, "Yes, Jesus is important, but you also need this other teaching, this other practice, this other mediator." But the Bible says that Christ is all-sufficient. In Him dwells all the fullness of the Godhead bodily (Col. 2:9). He is the only mediator between God and men (1 Tim. 2:5). There is no other name under heaven given among men by which we must be saved (Acts 4:12).

Whoever has the Son has the Father also. This is a direct refutation of any teaching that separates Jesus from the Father or diminishes His deity. The Jehovah's Witnesses, for example, teach that Jesus is a created being, the first and greatest of God's creations, but not God Himself. The Mormons teach that Jesus is the spirit brother of Lucifer, one of many spirit children of Heavenly Father. The Muslims honor Jesus as a prophet but deny that He is the Son of God.

All of these systems claim to honor God, but they do not have God, because they reject the true Christ. They have invented a different Jesus—a Jesus who did not rise bodily from the dead, or a Jesus who is not fully God, or a Jesus who is one of many ways to heaven. But that Jesus cannot save. Only the Jesus of Scripture, the Jesus who is fully God and fully man, the Jesus who died for our sins and rose again on the third day, can save.

The Command: Do Not Receive False Teachers

> *"If anyone comes to you and does not bring this doctrine, do not receive him into your house nor greet him; for he who greets him shares in his evil deeds." (2 John 10-11)*

This is one of the most controversial commands in the New Testament, and it must be understood in context. John is not saying that we should be rude to unbelievers or refuse to show basic human kindness to those who are lost. What he is addressing is the practice, common in the first century, of welcoming traveling teachers into your home, providing them with food and lodging, and then sending them on their way with a blessing and financial support.

In the early church, there were many itinerant preachers and teachers who traveled from city to city, proclaiming the gospel and teaching the churches. They depended on the hospitality of believers for their survival. When a traveling teacher arrived, a local believer would take them in, feed them, house them, and then send them off with provisions for the next leg of their journey. This was considered a ministry of support, and those who did it were viewed as partners in the work of the gospel.

But John says: If the teacher is teaching false doctrine, do not extend this hospitality. Do not receive them into your house. Do not support them. Do not send them on their way with your blessing. Why? Because if you do, you become a partaker in their evil deeds. By supporting a false teacher, you are helping to spread false doctrine. You are enabling them to deceive others. You are, in effect, partnering with them in their work of destruction.

The phrase "nor greet him" literally means "do not bid him God speed." In other words, do not send him off with a blessing like, "Go with God" or "May the Lord bless your journey." Why? Because you do not want God to bless a mission of deception. You do not want to invoke God's favor on someone who is teaching lies about God's Son.

Interestingly, the English word "goodbye" is derived from the phrase "God be with you." Over time, this phrase was contracted into "Godbwye," and eventually "goodbye." So when John says not to bid them God speed, he is essentially saying, "Don't even say goodbye in a way that invokes God's blessing on their work."

Now, does this mean we cannot invite Mormons or Jehovah's Witnesses into our home to share the gospel with them? Of course not. The difference is intent. If you are inviting them in to evangelize them, to lovingly but firmly show them the truth and call them to repentance and faith in the true Christ, that is entirely different from providing them with support and endorsement as they go out to deceive others.

234

In fact, one pastor used to follow the Mormons around his neighborhood. Whenever they knocked on someone's door, he would stand right there with them and politely but firmly explain to his neighbors that what the Mormons were teaching was false. He would say, "These are my neighbors, and this is my town, and I'm not going to let false doctrine be spread here unchallenged." Was he being unloving? No. He was protecting the sheep. He was guarding the truth. He was doing exactly what a faithful shepherd should do.

John's command is about partnership, not about basic human decency. We can be kind to false teachers. We can pray for their salvation. We can seek opportunities to share the truth with them. But we must not support their ministries. We must not endorse their teaching. We must not give them a platform or provide them with resources to spread their lies. To do so would be to become complicit in leading people away from Christ.

The True Doctrine: Jesus Is God

So what is the true doctrine of Christ? What must we believe? At the heart of Christian orthodoxy is the doctrine of the Trinity: God exists as three persons—Father, Son, and Holy Spirit—yet He is one God, not three gods. Each person is fully God, co-equal, co-eternal, and co-essential. This is the faith that was once for all delivered to the saints (Jude 3).

The early church wrestled with how to articulate this doctrine in the face of various heresies. In AD 313, the Emperor Constantine issued the Edict of Milan, which granted religious tolerance to Christians and ended centuries of persecution. For the first time, believers could worship openly without fear of arrest, torture, or execution.

But with this newfound freedom came a new challenge: false teaching began to spread more easily.

A man named Arius began teaching that Jesus was not truly God, but rather the first and greatest of God's creations. This heresy, known as Arianism, gained a wide following and threatened to split the church. In response, church leaders from across the known world gathered in AD 325 at the Council of Nicaea to settle the matter. The result was the Nicene Creed, a clear statement of what Christians believe about the nature of God and the person of Christ.

Later, the church formulated the Apostles' Creed, a shorter and simpler summary of the faith. Many churches recite this creed regularly as a reminder of the essentials. It reads:

I believe in God, the Father almighty, creator of heaven and earth. I believe in Jesus Christ, his only Son, our Lord, who was conceived by the Holy Spirit and born of the virgin Mary. He suffered under Pontius Pilate, was crucified, died, and was buried; he descended to hell. The third day he rose again from the dead. He ascended to heaven and is seated at the right hand of God the Father almighty. From there he will come to judge the living and the dead. I believe in the Holy Spirit, the holy universal church, the communion of saints, the forgiveness of sins, the resurrection of the body, and the life everlasting. Amen.

Notice the phrase "his only Son." This directly refutes the Mormon teaching that Jesus is one of many spirit children of Heavenly Father, with Lucifer being His spirit brother. No. Jesus is the only begotten Son of God. He is unique. He is singular. There is no one like Him.

After the Apostles' Creed, another creed was developed to more fully explain the doctrine of the Trinity. Known as the Athanasian Creed, it is attributed to Athanasius, a young theologian who was present at the Council of Nicaea and who spent much of his life defending the deity of Christ. While the creed is lengthy, its core message is clear:

Whoever desires to be saved must above all hold to the universal faith. Anyone who does not keep it whole and unbroken will doubtless perish eternally. Now this is the universal faith: that we worship one God in Trinity and the Trinity in unity, neither blending their persons nor dividing their essence. The Father, Son, and Holy Spirit are each distinct persons, but altogether one. Their glory is equal, their majesty co-eternal.

The creed goes on to affirm that the Father, the Son, and the Holy Spirit are each uncreated, immeasurable, eternal, almighty, God, and Lord. Yet there are not three gods, but one God. Each person of the Trinity is fully God, yet there is only one God.

The creed also addresses the incarnation:

It is necessary for eternal salvation that one also believe in the incarnation of our Lord Jesus Christ faithfully. Now this is the true faith: that we believe and confess that our Lord Jesus Christ, God's Son, is both God and human, equally. He is God from the essence of the Father, begotten before time; and He is human from the essence of His mother, born in time. Completely God, completely human, with a rational soul and human flesh. Equal to the Father as regards divinity, less than the Father as regards humanity.

This is the mystery of the incarnation: Jesus is fully God and fully man. He is not half God and half man. He is not a man who became God, nor is He God merely pretending to be a man. He is the eternal Son of God who took on human flesh, lived a sinless life, died an atoning death, and rose

237

again in victory. And He remains both God and man forevermore.

Although He is God and human, yet Christ is not two, but one. He is one, however, not by His divinity being turned into flesh, but by God taking humanity to Himself. He is one, certainly not by the blending of His essence, but by the unity of His person. For just as one human is both rational soul and flesh, so too the one Christ is both God and human.

The creed concludes: This is the universal faith. One cannot be saved without believing it firmly and faithfully.

Now, some may object that this sounds harsh. Are we really saying that someone who does not understand the Trinity cannot be saved? We must be careful here. Salvation is by grace through faith in Jesus Christ, not by perfect theological understanding. A new believer may not yet grasp the full doctrine of the Trinity, but as they grow, they will come to see it in Scripture and embrace it.

What the creed is condemning is not ignorance, but willful rejection of the truth. It is one thing to struggle to understand a complex doctrine. It is quite another to be taught the truth and then deliberately deny it. The Jehovah's Witnesses have been taught that Jesus is God, but they reject it. The Mormons have been taught that there is one God in three persons, but they reject it. And in rejecting the true Christ, they reject the only Savior who can save them.

The Heart of the Gospel: All About Jesus

At the close of his letter, John writes:

> *"Having many things to write to you, I did not wish to do so with paper and ink; but I*

hope to come to you and speak face to face,
that our joy may be full. The children of
your elect sister greet you. Amen."
(2 John 12-13)

John prefers face-to-face conversation to writing. There is wisdom in this. Some conversations are simply too important, too nuanced, or too sensitive to be handled through written correspondence. Body language, tone of voice, and the ability to immediately clarify misunderstandings all make face-to-face communication far superior for certain topics.

In our modern age of texting and social media, we would do well to remember this. Not everything should be said in a text message. Some conversations require a phone call. Some require sitting down together over coffee. Some require looking someone in the eye and speaking with both truth and love.

Before we close, there is one more critical truth that must be emphasized, and it comes from the words of the great preacher Charles Spurgeon: "This is the doctrine that we preach: if a man be saved, all the honor is to be given to Christ. But if a man be lost, all the blame is to be laid upon himself."

This is the heart of the gospel. Salvation is all of grace. We contribute nothing. We bring nothing to the table except our sin, our guilt, and our need. And Jesus provides everything else. He lived the perfect life we could not live. He died the atoning death we deserved to die. He rose from the grave in victory over sin and death. And He offers us forgiveness, righteousness, and eternal life as a free gift, received by faith alone.

If this gospel you are hearing is not all about Jesus and His completed work, then it is a false gospel. Any system that adds human works, human merit, or human effort to the finished work of Christ is not the gospel of grace. It is another gospel, which is really no gospel at all (Gal. 1:6-7).

The Mormons teach that you can work your way up to higher levels of heaven. The Roman Catholics teach that you must participate in the sacraments and cooperate with grace to be saved. The Jehovah's Witnesses teach that only 144,000 will go to heaven, and the rest will live forever on a paradise earth if they are faithful. Many other groups add their own requirements: baptism in their church, speaking in tongues, keeping the Sabbath, abstaining from certain foods, and on and on.

But the gospel of Jesus Christ says: Come as you are. Come with your sin. Come with your shame. Come with your failure. Come with your brokenness. And He will give you what you do not deserve and could never earn. He will give you forgiveness. He will give you righteousness. He will give you eternal life. Not because you are good, but because He is good. Not because you are worthy, but because He is gracious.

When I realize that I could never earn my salvation, it makes me appreciate Him all the more. It makes me worship Him with all my heart. It makes me want to live for Him, not out of fear or obligation, but out of love and gratitude. I am saved, and I did nothing to deserve it. All the glory goes to Him.

Now, if you are reading this and you are not yet certain of your salvation, let me emphasize one more time: No one is getting kicked out of heaven because they misunderstood a doctrine. Salvation is not about having perfect theology. It is about trusting in a perfect Savior. But the churches and teachers who plainly and persistently deny the core truths of the gospel—who teach a different Jesus, a different God, a different way of salvation—they are leading people to destruction.

If you have been deceived by false teaching, it is not too late. Turn to the true Christ. The Jesus of the Bible, who is fully God and fully man, who died for sinners and rose again, who saves by grace alone through faith alone. Trust in Him. Rest in His finished work. And you will be saved.

And for those of us who know the truth, we have a responsibility. We must contend earnestly for the faith (Jude 3). We must be ready to give an answer for the hope that is in us (1 Pet. 3:15). We must guard the truth, teach the truth, and live the truth. And we must do so with both conviction and compassion, with both boldness and love.

As Jude wrote, and as we echo in our own hearts:

> *"Now to Him who is able to keep you from*
> *stumbling, and to present you faultless*
> *before the presence of His glory with*
> *exceeding joy, to God our Savior, who alone*
> *is wise, be glory and majesty, dominion and*
> *power, both now and forever. Amen."*
> *(Jude 24-25)*

Let us together worship one God in Trinity and the Trinity in unity, neither blending their persons nor dividing their essence. Let us hold fast to the truth. Let us love one another. And let us contend earnestly for the faith that was once for all delivered to the saints.

The Epistles of John

Spiritual Health
3 John

Introduction

Third John is the smallest book of the Bible when counting words rather than verses. Though it contains more verses, in the Greek, 3 John has 219 words versus 2 John, which has 245. Despite its brevity, this final epistle of John is packed with wisdom and application for the church today.

As background to the epistles of John, it is worth noting that John wrote his Gospel and three epistles after penning the book of Revelation. While in his late 80s, serving as pastor of the church at Ephesus, Caesar Domitian had John exiled to the island of Patmos. There, Jesus appeared to him, and John recorded what became the book of Revelation. After returning from exile, John wrote his Gospel and epistles, making 3 John likely the last book of the Bible to be written.

John died around the year AD 100—some 70 years after the crucifixion. Tradition places him in his 90s at death, which helps explain why many scholars believe John was quite young at the time of the crucifixion, perhaps in his early 20s or even late teens. The older John was at the crucifixion, the older he would have been at death, and we know he lived over 70 years beyond that pivotal event.

As John calls himself "the elder" in this letter, the reader should remember this is a very old man writing with the weight of decades of ministry and the authority of the last living apostle. By this time, John had become known for his emphasis on love—his final messages to the churches often consisted simply of exhorting believers to "love one another."

More Is Caught Than Taught

The book of 3 John contains valuable lessons about parenting, marriage, and spiritual leadership that are worth emphasizing. The principle that more is caught than taught applies powerfully here. Little eyes are watching. Friends are watching. People are watching. It has been said that you are the fifth gospel—people won't read Matthew, Mark, Luke, and John, but they will read you and watch your life to see how you are living. That will preach to them.

Parents cannot tell their children one thing and then live another way. Likewise, believers cannot preach one thing to others while living differently themselves. The walk must match the talk. John's joy in hearing that his spiritual children walk in truth demonstrates this principle perfectly.

"The elder, to the beloved Gaius, whom I love in truth." (3 John 1)

John writes to "the beloved Gaius, whom I love in truth." There are a few men named Gaius mentioned in the New Testament—one from Corinth and one from Derbe appear in the book of Acts. However, the way John speaks of this Gaius is similar to how Paul speaks of Timothy as "my son in the faith." John seems to have a special connection with this Gaius, leading many to believe that Gaius was one of John's converts, which would make him yet another Gaius, distinct from those mentioned elsewhere in Scripture.

In verse 2, John writes:

> *"Beloved, I pray that you may prosper in all things and be in health, just as your soul prospers." (3 John 2)*

Some have taken this verse out of context to support a prosperity gospel, suggesting that Christians should be prospering materially. However, the idea here is simply that John is offering a general blessing and introduction. He knows the strength of Gaius's spiritual health and simply expresses hope that God will bless him materially and physically as well. It is a heartfelt wish for his wellbeing.

In the Roman world, prosperity and health were common greetings in letters—much like how Paul and Peter often used "grace and peace" as a Christian introduction. In fact, these phrases were so common that they would often be abbreviated in correspondence, similar to how modern letters might use "PS" for postscript or how people today use abbreviations like "TTYL" for "talk to you later." So there is no need to make too much of this greeting.

John continues in verse 3:

> *"For I rejoiced greatly when brethren came and testified of the truth that is in you, just as you walk in the truth. I have no greater joy than to hear that my children walk in truth." (3 John 3-4)*

In this little book of 14 verses, the word "truth" appears in five verses, six times total. John emphasizes that Gaius is in the truth, walking in the truth, and that John has, "no greater joy than to hear that his children walk in truth."

This verse—3 John 4—has become my life verse. When first saved, my life verse was 2 Corinthians 5:17: "Therefore, if anyone is in Christ, he is a new creation; old things have passed away; behold, all things have become new." That verse provided the reassurance I needed early in my Christian walk. But as one matures in ministry and begins pastoring a church, verse 4 takes on profound meaning: "I have no greater joy than to hear that my children walk in truth."

There is nothing in this world like the twofold joy of seeing one's own physical children doing well and seeing spiritual children—those discipled over the years—thriving in their faith. When believers are walking in power, walking in freedom, and doing well spiritually, it brings deep satisfaction. This is where John's heart was with Gaius. As an old man, John could say, "Yes, Gaius, it feels so good to hear that you are strong in your faith."

Notice that they are "walking in the truth," which is very different from simply believing the truth. James says, "You believe that there is one God. You do well. Even the demons believe—and tremble!" (James 2:19). James makes the point that demons believe in God, but they have not put their faith in God. There is a significant difference. God expects more than intellectual assent—more than just recognizing that there is a God.

A person can acknowledge the entire Nicene Creed or Apostles Creed and still not have saving faith. Evidence of true faith is often seen in whether people are walking in the truth. When believers walk in the truth, they have taken it, applied it, and are actually doing it.

It is one thing to say you believe something. It is another thing to act upon what you believe. Once, a member of our church came up and sat in a chair during the sermon, and the congregation applauded—but she was confused because all she did was sit down. The point was this: she demonstrated perfect faith in that chair. She did not shake it or kick it to test it; she simply believed the chair would hold her and sat on it. That is how faith works. When people truly believe something, they naturally act upon it because they really believe.

If someone claimed to have a pet tarantula and said, "You can pet it; it doesn't bite," many would reply, "I believe you"—but they would not get anywhere near petting it. That is how some people's faith operates. They say they believe, but they are afraid to act upon it. If we say we believe there is a fire in the kids ministry yet no one gets up to save the children, do we really believe there is a fire? Walking in the truth means acting on what we believe.

Three Examples: Two Good and One Bad

Beginning in verse 5, John presents three examples: two good men and one bad man. Two positive examples and one negative example.

> *"Beloved, you do faithfully whatever you do for the brethren and for strangers, who have borne witness of your love before the church. If you send them forward on their journey in a manner worthy of God, you will do well, because they went forth for His name's sake, taking nothing from the Gentiles. We therefore ought to receive such, that we may become fellow workers for the truth. I wrote to the church, but Diotrephes, who loves to have the preeminence among them, does not receive us. Therefore, if I come, I will call to mind his deeds which he does, prating against us with malicious words. And not content with that, he himself does not receive the*

> *brethren, and forbids those who wish to,*
> *putting them out of the church."*
> *(3 John 5-10)*

This passage addresses the topic of welcoming people into the church—specifically, welcoming traveling teachers, preachers, apostles, and prophets. In those days, these ministers would travel from place to place, needing housing and food. Gaius excelled at providing this hospitality.

This connects to the teaching on the body of Christ in Ephesians 4:11-16, where Paul explains that the whole body has been given gifts to minister to one another, building each other up so that believers have the power and strength to pour into other people. Everyone has different gifts and a different part in the body.

Gaius appears to be a leader in his church, though perhaps not the pastor. Diotrephes may have been the pastor, though this is uncertain. What is clear is that Gaius led well. His specific contribution was welcoming and caring for traveling ministers—even strangers. He did not know them personally, but he knew they were serving the Lord, so he cared for them.

Whatever You Do, Do It Faithfully

Verse 5 says, "Beloved, you do faithfully whatever you do." This can be rearranged into a powerful exhortation: Whatever you do, do it faithfully.

Believers have been given gifts. They are fearfully and wonderfully made to be a part in the body of Christ. There are no vestigial organs in the body of Christ. Everyone has a role and a function, and it is important to the body. Whatever that role is, it should be done faithfully.

The fingernail might look at the hand and think, "I wish I were the whole hand." But the fingernail should not sit there wishing it were the hand. It should be a fingernail. The hand needs the fingernail for protection. The fingernail has a job—do it faithfully.

In Matthew 25, Jesus tells the parable of the talents. A master leaves and gives one servant five talents, another two talents, and another one talent. When the master returns, the servant with five talents has turned them into ten. Matthew 25:21 records the master's response:

> *"His lord said to him, 'Well done, good and faithful servant; you were faithful over a few things, I will make you ruler over many things. Enter into the joy of your lord.'"* *(Matt. 25:21)*

The servant with two talents had turned his into four, also doubling what he was given. In verse 23, Jesus gives the exact same reward and commendation:

> *"His lord said to him, 'Well done, good and faithful servant; you have been faithful over a few things, I will make you ruler over many things. Enter into the joy of your lord.'"* *(Matt. 25:23)*

The exact same reward. One servant had ten talents, but he was given more to begin with. From the parable, we understand that to whom much is given, much will be required. It does not matter what role one has in the body of Christ. What matters is: Are you being faithful with what God has given you? The commendation is not "Well done, good and talented servant." It is "Well done, good and *faithful* servant."

So Gaius is commended: "Beloved, you do faithfully whatever you do." What exactly was he doing? He was taking in traveling ministers. These ministers would travel without lodging. Most inns and taverns in that era were also brothels—places where travelers could get drunk and hire prostitutes. Christians traveling did not want to stay in those places. They looked for the hospitality of fellow believers, trying to find the church in each town to see if someone would take them in.

This was very normal in the first and second centuries as the church was spreading. One of the earliest Christian writings outside the New Testament is called the Didache, which literally means "the teaching." Tradition holds that it is the teaching of the apostles—a document they created to instruct new churches. Chapter 11 of the Didache addresses this very issue of hosting traveling ministers:

> "Let every apostle that comes to you be received as the Lord. But he shall not remain except one day; but if there be need, also the next; but if he remain three days, he is a false prophet. And when the apostle goes away, let him take nothing but bread until he lodges. But if he ask money, he is a false prophet... And every prophet who orders a meal in the Spirit eats not from it, except indeed he be a false prophet; and every prophet who teaches the truth, if he do not what he teaches, is a false prophet."

The Didache warned against prophets who would say, "The Lord is telling me today is the day we slay the fatted calf"—a prophet looking for personal benefit. If a prophet truly received a word from the Lord, he would not eat of it himself. The Didache simply states: "A prophet who teaches the truth, if he does not do what he teaches, is a false prophet."

2 John and 3 John both deal with traveling teachers— determining whether they are legitimate or not. If they are legitimate, take care of them. If they are not legitimate, do not even let them into your home, as 2 John instructs. Here, John encourages Gaius to keep the hospitality going. At the end of verse 8, John writes that by doing so, "we may become fellow workers for the truth."

This is important to understand: Gaius may not have been the one teaching people. The focus is on Gaius caring for the teachers. By caring for the teachers, Gaius became a partaker of the reward and of the work. He was part of what was going on.

Ephesians 4:16 teaches:

> *"from whom the whole body, joined and knit together by what every joint supplies, according to the effective working by which every part does its share, causes growth of the body for the edifying of itself in love."*
> *(Eph. 4:16)*

It takes a whole body to make a healthy body. It takes all the parts of the body doing their share to see a powerful church. Not everyone can be on the front lines because someone must support those on the front lines. Not everyone could be a missionary because someone must support the missionaries so they can be out there.

If believers give to their local church, they are supporting missionaries. They are giving to missions in other countries, to short-term and long-term missionaries. We are all part of that work. In 1 Samuel 30, the Amalekites take all the gold, women, and children from David's men.

251

The Epistles of John

David's men pursue them, but some cannot keep going, so David tells them to stay back and guard the camp. When the enemy is defeated and the goods are recovered, some do not want to share with those who stayed behind. But David says:

> *"For as his share is who goes down to the battle, so shall his share be who stays by the supplies; they shall share alike." (1 Sam. 30:24)*

The next verse notes that this became a statute in Israel. The person on the front lines and the person on the back lines are rewarded the same. Some need to be on the front lines with weapons. Some need to be on the back lines preparing food for the soldiers. Without cooks and mechanics, an army dies. Without support, those on the front lines cannot function.

Here is the simple connection: We are all partaking in the work. One way to do it is by supporting people on the front lines. For example, a local church pays someone to mow the lawn so the pastor can study, meet with couples for counseling, and pray. In Acts 6, when people came to the apostles with needs, they responded:

> *"Therefore, brethren, seek out from among you seven men of good reputation, full of the Holy Spirit and wisdom, whom we may appoint over this business; but we will give ourselves continually to prayer and to the ministry of the word." (Acts 6:3-4)*

The apostles focused on the word and prayer. As believers volunteer and help, they offload others, allowing them to be more focused on their calling in the body of Christ. This is a beautiful picture of how "we may become fellow workers for the truth." We are all in it together. Some may never do street evangelism, but there are people who do, and there are ways to open doors to enable them. Some may never give directly to a missionary, but they can give through the church. It is a beautiful picture of partnership in the gospel.

The Bad Example: Diotrephes

The picture is not so beautiful when it comes to Diotrephes. In short, he is selfish. He wants the attention. He wants the preeminence. Verse 9 indicates that John wrote to the church—perhaps another letter—and it seems Diotrephes prevented the people from reading it. This man did not want other teachers in his church. He commanded the people not to take in itinerant preachers, and if people let them in, he kicked those people out of the church. Diotrephes was clearly in a position of authority and on a power trip.

John writes in verse 10, "Therefore, if I come, I will call to mind his deeds which he does." Even at 95 years old, there is still a son of thunder in John's heart.

Verse 11 transitions from the bad example back to positive instruction:

> *"Beloved, do not imitate what is evil, but*
> *what is good. He who does good is of God,*
> *but he who does evil has not seen God."*
> *(3 John 11)*

This is straightforward: By their fruit you shall know them. If people display bad fruit, it is unwise to follow them. If people display good fruit, hang around and follow those people. It has been said that it is easy to surround oneself with Christians, but what one ought to be doing is surrounding oneself with *godly* people—people who will have a positive impact on one's life because there is fruit.

"He who does good is of God. He who does evil has not seen God." This is not a law stating that Christians never do bad or always do good. But the general rule is true: when people live questionable lives with all bad fruit, it is reasonable to assume they are not truly Christians. The difference is in the response to sin. True Christians who fall into sin are broken-hearted and want to make it right. That is normal in the Christian walk. But when people are in sin and do not seem to care—that is bad fruit.

By their fruit you shall know them. When good fruit is present, it typically indicates who someone really is. When bad fruit is present, it reveals the same.

The Second Good Example: Demetrius

John mentions Demetrius, the second good model:

> *"Demetrius has a good testimony from all, and from the truth itself. And we also bear witness, and you know that our testimony is true." (3 John 12)*

This is vague, but the point is clear: Demetrius has a good testimony from all. If you line his life up with the word of God, it looks good. John affirms him. It is likely that in the letter John mentioned in verse 9, there were questions or negative things said about Demetrius by Diotrephes or others, and John is writing to settle it: He is legitimate. Do not listen to Diotrephes or anyone else who says otherwise.

We do not know much about Demetrius other than that he is a good man with a credible testimony.

Closing Exhortations

Verses 13 and 14 provide practical nuggets:

> *"I had many things to write, but I do not*
> *wish to write to you with pen and ink; but I*
> *hope to see you shortly, and we shall speak*
> *face to face. Peace to you. Our friends greet*
> *you. Greet the friends by name."*
> *(3 John 13-14)*

First, "Greet the friends by name." It is good to learn people's names. Get to know new people. Say their name again and again. Do whatever it takes, because it shows care. John does not just say, "Tell everyone I said hi." He is specific: Make sure individuals hear the greeting personally.

Second, "I do not wish to write to you, but hope to speak face to face." This is practical wisdom. In this age, everyone is busy and rushed, and it is convenient to shoot someone a text. But there is a lot that is not good over text. If a serious conversation is needed, it should be face to face. When speaking face to face, if something comes out wrong, it can be corrected immediately. Communication is clearer eye to eye. In the Greek, it is literally "mouth to mouth"—direct, personal communication.

Spiritual Health

Verse 4 is powerful: "I have no greater joy than to hear that my children walk in truth." But the more time spent on that verse, the more verse 2 became compelling:

> *"Beloved, I pray that you may prosper in all*
> *things and be in health, just as your soul*
> *prospers." (3 John 2)*

The reality is that most people today—unless in very poor physical health—might think their physical health and material prosperity are doing better than their soul. Spiritual health might not be as strong as what they are doing physically and materially. Yet spiritual health is critically important for the church.

So the question arises: What is needed to be healthy? This can be tied to physical health, and there are many connections. God made it easy for us to understand.

Food and Shelter: The Basics

To survive at the bare minimum, we need food and shelter. If lost in the woods for an extended time, what is needed first? Food and shelter. Protection from the elements is essential, which is why clothing is included. Everything in the environment is trying to harm—whether sun, cold, heat, or weather. So food and clothing are needed, and typically a building for housing and protection from the elements.

Paul summarizes this in 1 Timothy 6:8:

> *"And having food and clothing, with these we shall be content." (1 Tim. 6:8)*

Paul recognized that to maintain any kind of life at all, these two things are needed.

Spiritual Food

Psalm 34:8 says, "Oh, taste and see that the LORD is good." Believers should be consuming the Lord, taking Him in. The easiest way to do that is through His word. Jesus told Satan during the temptation in the wilderness:

> *"It is written, 'Man shall not live by bread*
> *alone, but by every word that proceeds from*
> *the mouth of God.'" (Matt. 4:4)*

Throughout the New Testament, the word of God is described as "the milk of the word" and "the meat of the word"—nourishment. We consume it regularly, and it brings spiritual health. Some people wonder why they feel great after church but struggle the rest of the week. They came to church and got a good meal. But are they eating breakfast on Monday? If someone only ate one day a week, they would lose weight rapidly and in a very unhealthy way.

Jesus, in the Bread of Life discourse in John 6, said:

> *"I am the living bread which came down*
> *from heaven. If anyone eats of this bread, he*
> *will live forever." (John 6:51)*

If believers want to be spiritually strong, they need to be consuming God's word on a regular basis. Daily engagement with Scripture is essential for spiritual health and strength.

Spiritual Shelter

Whether clothing or a building, shelter creates a barrier from outside elements that are dangerous. For spiritual protection and shelter, there is nothing better than the church—not just a building, but when surrounded by believers, there is protection. There is a surrounding that keeps us safe from all the things out there trying to harm.

Hebrews 10:24-25 teaches:

> *"And let us consider one another in order to*
> *stir up love and good works, not forsaking*

> *the assembling of ourselves together, as is*
> *the manner of some, but exhorting one*
> *another, and so much the more as you see*
> *the Day approaching." (Heb. 10:24-25)*

The word "consider" means to really look at and examine someone. This cannot be done over the phone—only face to face. When we look at someone and consider them, we can realize this person needs some love and good works stirred up. And we are not to forsake assembling together, but to exhort one another all the more as the Day approaches.

If we believe we are living in the last days, we should be surrounding ourselves with believers all the more—godly people surrounding us.

There are things people could say or do at work or with family members that no one would care about or think is sinful—kind of petty sins. Yet the exact same behavior or words around Christian friends would prompt someone to say something: "What's up with that? Why are you acting that way? Why are you talking that way?" As we surround ourselves with godly people, we find ourselves becoming less like the world and more like the church, more like Christ.

Exercise and Rest: Exceptional Health

To move beyond survival to exceptional health, we add exercise and rest. Rest is often forgotten. God gave the Sabbath for a reason—people will work themselves around the clock if not told to rest. While Christians apply the Sabbath differently, the principle remains: we need rest.

A common mistake for those new to the gym is working the same muscles every day without rest. The muscles never recover and grow because they are constantly torn down. Muscles need rest to grow.

Prayer as Exercise

John Calvin said, "Prayer is the chief exercise of faith." There are many exercises believers can do. Paul said bodily exercise profits a little, but godliness is profitable for all things (1 Tim. 4:8). We exercise ourselves in godliness. Prayer is exercising what we know in our minds. We know the word of God. How do we put this into action? We need to remember that there are promises in the word of God and warnings in the word. If we want to use those promises, we must talk to God.

Consider the account in Daniel where Daniel prays and God sends an angel. The angel is stopped by a demon, and they fight until Michael helps. When the angel finally arrives, he tells Daniel, *"The moment you prayed, I was sent."*

Why didn't God just send the angel before Daniel prayed? God knew what was coming. But that is not how it works. The angel was ready to go, just waiting for the call. That is how God operates. He has laid it down: You pray and ask for these things, and I am not going to give it until you ask.

Any parent has done this with their kids—seeing them struggle but not stepping in until they ask. We let them fight it out on their own until they come and ask.

Another reason prayer is exercise: Anyone who has done exercise knows what it is like to be in shape and out of shape. When trying to return to old performance levels after being out of shape, it is difficult. Spiritual fitness works the same way. When spiritually out of shape, it is hard to pray and spend real time in prayer. But as the discipline is exercised and prayer increases, the ability to pray grows. Strength in prayer is built.

A young man from our church, who a couple years earlier was a pothead in all sorts of trouble, recently shared that one hour of prayer is not enough—he has reached a place where an hour goes by and he still wants to pray. Both he and his pastor know what that feels like, where the desire to pray is strong and time flies. Both also know what it feels like when it is not that way—when getting 15 minutes of sincere prayer without the mind wandering or wanting to quit feels like pulling teeth. There is being in shape and being out of shape. Prayer is exercise.

Leonard Ravenhill addressed this:

> *"Don't go out and say like people say, 'Well, I've made up my mind and I am going to start praying for hours a day after this.' Why don't you make your mind up that you are going to run in the Olympics tomorrow?"*

Ravenhill pointed out that it is just as foolish to think one can develop deep spirituality overnight and become a prayer warrior by flipping a switch as it is to think one can run in the Olympics without training. But if one commits and trains and exercises that discipline, endurance will be built through prayer.

You will never grow if your prayer life does not grow. That is a fact. It is connected to spiritual health and maturity. Your faith will suffer if your prayer life suffers.

As newborn believers, it is critical to get into the word so they know what they believe and why they believe it. But as people mature, their devotional life should shift, with more and more time being put into prayer. Not that the word is dropped or reading stops, but proportionally, the prayer side should grow.

Rest and Peace

Rest is critically important. Peace and rest are what we want in this world. Jeremiah says to the people of Israel:

> *"Thus says the LORD: 'Stand in the ways and see, and ask for the old paths, where the good way is, and walk in it; then you will find rest for your souls.' But they said, 'We will not walk in it.'" (Jer. 6:16)*

That is a Hebrew word for literally a crossroad—a Y in the road. Stand at that crossroad. You get to choose which road to go down from there forward. Ask for the old paths, where the good way is, and walk in it. Then you will find rest for your souls. The people replied to Jeremiah, "We will not walk in it."

Many people probably know what they need to be doing. But they have to choose at the crossroad whether to start going down that path.

In Luke 10, Jesus speaks to Martha:

> *"Martha, Martha, you are worried and troubled about many things. But one thing is needed, and Mary has chosen that good part, which will not be taken away from her." (Luke 10:41-42)*

Martha is worried. The Greek word is *merimnao* (μεριμνάω), a broad word translated into English as "care," "worry," or "anxiety." Martha is anxious about day-to-day things—getting food ready, getting everything prepared. Jesus is saying, "You are worried about so much, Martha.

You are missing out on what Mary is doing—just sitting at My feet, knowing Me and loving Me."

In Luke 8, in the parable of the sower, Jesus describes the third soil:

> *"Now the ones that fell among thorns are*
> *those who, when they have heard, go out*
> *and are choked with cares, riches, and*
> *pleasures of life, and bring no fruit to*
> *maturity." (Luke 8:14)*

Merimna—the same word. "Cares." Christians bringing no fruit to maturity because they are getting choked to death by worries, anxieties, and fears. This is the opposite of peace and rest. If there is peace and rest, worries and anxieties are the opposite.

So what do we do? First Peter 5:7: *"casting all your care upon Him, for He cares for you." (1 Pet. 5:7)*

Same word—*merimna*. We are supposed to cast all these things upon Him. How? Philippians 4:6-7:

> *"Be anxious for nothing, but in everything*
> *by prayer and supplication, with*
> *thanksgiving, let your requests be made*
> *known to God; and the peace of God, which*
> *surpasses all understanding, will guard your*
> *hearts and minds through Christ Jesus."*
> *(Phil. 4:6-7)*

Same word again. Be anxious—*merimnao*—for nothing. Never be worried or anxious about anything. But in everything, in all that you do in life, by prayer and supplication (asking for supplies—requesting) and with thanksgiving, let your requests be known to God.

Prayer means talking to God. Supplication means asking for supplies—the requesting part. And thanksgiving. If we have kids, we are familiar with being asked a lot. Isn't it nice when there is a little thanksgiving? Maybe if we did a little more thanksgiving with our prayers and supplications, God would help change our minds about things, because we would realize all the good things we had to be thankful for.

If we start praying about things, the promise is that the peace of God, which surpasses understanding, will guard our hearts and minds through Christ Jesus. God will bring us peace.

Jesus says in John 14:27:

> *"Peace I leave with you, My peace I give to you; not as the world gives do I give to you. Let not your heart be troubled, neither let it be afraid." (John 14:27)*

The world offers many things, claiming they will bring happiness: "If only I could get this, then I will finally be happy." That is the lie of Satan that has duped all of us at least once, if not a hundred times. "This thing will bring me peace." No, it will not. Read the book of Ecclesiastes. That is the whole book. "Vanity, vanity, vanity, vanity." Solomon says, "I tried everything, and it was all just vanity. You want to know the whole matter summed up? Fear God, obey His commands." Those are the last two verses of the book. He tried it all. Nothing in this world gave him peace. God will give you peace.

It is good to know that there is not just peace in this world—the peace of God—but also peace

with God. Isaiah 53:6:

> *"All we like sheep have gone astray; we*
> *have turned, every one, to his own way; and*
> *the LORD has laid on Him the iniquity of us*
> *all." (Isa. 53:6)*

It is all about Jesus and what He has done for us. He laid on Him the iniquity of us all. We are saved by grace through faith (Eph. 2:8). Romans 5:1 says:

> *"Therefore, having been justified by faith,*
> *we have peace with God through our Lord*
> *Jesus Christ." (Rom. 5:1)*

Satan will try to make us think we have lost it, or let it go, or are not good enough, or this or that. We memorize these verses: "Lord, it is all about You. It was never about me in the first place. I was saved through faith. And since I have been justified by faith, that is why I have peace with God—not because of my performance." We need to remember God's promises and His word when Satan is trying to challenge us and get us to doubt.

Jesus' words in Matthew 11:28-30 close this out beautifully:

> *"Come to Me, all you who labor and are*
> *heavy laden, and I will give you rest. Take*
> *My yoke upon you and learn from Me, for I*
> *am gentle and lowly in heart, and you will*
> *find rest for your souls. For My yoke is easy*
> *and My burden is light." (Matt. 11:28-30)*

If we want to be healthy, we need to be experiencing the peace and rest of God. If somehow religion feels heavy, then that is what it is—religion, not His. Because Jesus says, "My yoke is easy and My burden is light. All I do is take burdens off of people. I take those burdens off of people and free them so they can live for Me."

As John closes out the final book written in Scripture, he has no greater joy than to hear his children walk in truth. As we have examined God's truth, may we be able to walk in God's truth and may our souls prosper.